THE SIGNIFICANCE IMPULSE

THE SIGNIFICANCE IMPULSE

On the Unimportance of Our Cosmic Unimportance

Joshua Glasgow

Oxford University Press is a department of the University of Oxford.
It furthers the University's objective of excellence in research, scholarship,
and education by publishing worldwide. Oxford is a registered trade mark of
Oxford University Press in the UK and in certain other countries.

Published in the United States of America by Oxford University Press
198 Madison Avenue, New York, NY 10016, United States of America.

© Oxford University Press 2024

All rights reserved. No part of this publication may be reproduced, stored in a retrieval system,
or transmitted, in any form or by any means, without the prior permission in writing of Oxford
University Press, or as expressly permitted by law, by license or under terms agreed with the
appropriate reprographics rights organization. Inquiries concerning reproduction outside the scope
of the above should be sent to the Rights Department, Oxford University Press, at the address above.

You must not circulate this work in any other form
and you must impose this same condition on any acquirer

Library of Congress Cataloging-in-Publication Data
Names: Glasgow, Joshua, author.
Title: The significance impulse : on the unimportance of our cosmic unimportance / Joshua Glasgow.
Description: New York, NY, United States of America : Oxford University Press, [2024] |
Includes bibliographical references.
Identifiers: LCCN 2024022917 (print) | LCCN 2024022918 (ebook) | ISBN 9780197754757 (hardback) |
ISBN 9780197754764 | ISBN 9780197754788 | ISBN 9780197754771 (epub)
Subjects: LCSH: Success. | Self-acceptance. | Happiness.
Classification: LCC BF637.S8 G5335 2024 (print) | LCC BF637.S8 (ebook) |
DDC 128—dc23/eng/20240801
LC record available at https://lccn.loc.gov/2024022917
LC ebook record available at https://lccn.loc.gov/2024022918

DOI: 10.1093/9780197754788.001.0001

Printed by Integrated Books International, United States of America

CONTENTS

Acknowledgments | vii

1. The Splinter and the Dove | 1

2. Value Rare and High | 14

3. The Sage's Argument | 23

4. Living Your Best Life | 48

5. Meaning | 69

6. The Significance of Insignificance | 93

REFERENCES | 111
INDEX | 121

ACKNOWLEDGMENTS

Material in Chapters 1, 2, and 5 was previously published as "The Ordinary Meaningful Life," in the *Journal of the American Philosophical Association* 9 (2023). Permission to reprint here is gratefully acknowledged.

Several people spent time and effort to assist me in getting this project off the ground, to discuss the issues explored in it, and to comment on earlier, less polished chunks of this book. Their generosity inspires and humbles me. For their help, I am grateful to Shani Long Abdallah, Jacob Affolter, Nick Agar, Sondra Bacharach, Ben Bradley, Stuart Brock, Kayla Brown, Cheshire Calhoun, Ramon Das, Matthew Hammerton, Terry Horgan, Guy Kahane, Simon Keller, Jeanette Kennett, Iddo Landau, Keith Lehrer, Catriona Mackenzie, Joan McGregor, Richard Menary, Kristi Mitrick, Julia Nefsky, Doug Portmore, Steven Reynolds, Rebecca Robinson, Lucy Schwarz, Lucas Scripter, Kieran Setiya, Julie Shulman, Saul Smilansky, Ikuro Suzuki, Justin Systyma, Mark Timmons, Manuel Vargas, and R. Jay Wallace.

Thanks also to anonymous referees at both Oxford University Press and the *Journal of the American Philosophical Association*, and Michael Hauskeller, for their helpful thoughts on earlier drafts, as well as to audiences for feedback provided at the 2016 American Philosophical Association Pacific Division, the First International

Conference on Philosophy and Meaning in Life, Arizona State University, Macquarie University, University of Arizona, and Victoria University of Wellington.

Finally, special appreciation goes to Lucy Randall and the rest of the team at Oxford University Press.

Even though this book argues that none of us are important on a larger scale, each of these people has been important to this project. Thank you, all, for your help.

1

The Splinter and the Dove

The baseball player Ted Williams famously said, "When I walk down the street and meet people, I just want them to think 'There goes the greatest hitter who ever lived.'" In actuality, the Splendid Splinter, as he was known, didn't just want people to *think* that he was the greatest hitter. He wanted people to *know* it—their belief grounded in the truth that he was, in fact, the greatest hitter who ever lived. Not to be outdone, Muhammad Ali once insisted, "I'm not the greatest. I'm the double greatest. Not only do I knock 'em out, I pick the round. I'm the boldest, the prettiest, the most superior, most scientific, most skillfullest fighter in the ring today." And, of course, these two are voicing a refrain familiar from a very wide range of endeavors. It is common to want to be great in some way—a Nobel-earning chemist, a three-star chef, an Oscar-winning actor. It is also common to covet important positions, such as member of Parliament or US president or, for the big dreamers, judge on *America's Got Talent*.

And it's not just that we want greatness for ourselves; at least in societies like mine, it is also common to tell your kids that they should strive to *be somebody*. It would make for an enviable life, we say. Many are raised to believe—not just by their parents but by the

The Significance Impulse. Joshua Glasgow, Oxford University Press. © Oxford University Press 2024.
DOI: 10.1093/9780197754788.003.0001

figures we lionize, the pursuits we glorify, the stories we repeat—that being truly important is good for us. People want to be special. They dream of being extraordinary. They think it would be in their self-interest if they were especially significant. Call this instinct the "Significance Impulse."

Making the big time promises to bring you money, fame, influence, and invitations to exclusive cocktail parties. But the Significance Impulse beats even more strongly than that. Apart from any downstream payoff that we might secure from being significant, many—like Teddy Ballgame—think that it also has its own value as a personal good. That is, even if you take away the instrumental value that being important can result in social rewards, being important is still thought to be in our interests. If you can one day be a Pulitzer Prize winner, you should go for it, not (just) for the financial, career, and social benefits but also (just) because being important makes for a better life than does a more pedestrian path, keeping all else equal. So says the Significance Impulse.

Now Williams wanted not only to *be* a great hitter but also to be *recognized* for being a great hitter. This desire for recognition is, like the desire for achieving significance, widespread: Tolstoy worried that he would at some point be forgotten, and in 23 B.C.E. Horace crowed that with his poetry "I have built a monument more lasting than bronze, higher than the Pyramids' regal structures, that no consuming rain, nor wild north wind can destroy."[1] We can draw a distinction between those two desires. The Significance Impulse values being *important,* not (or, rather, not *necessarily*) being *famous* or *rich* or *high-status* or otherwise socially recognized or rewarded for being important. The Impulse is not satisfied by the warped celebrity or the bloated banker whose notoriety outstrips what little value they might actually add to the world. In contrast to the drive to seek attention, wealth, or social approval, the Significance Impulse is only focused on actually adding extraordinary value to

1. Folger (2016).

the world, regardless of how or even *if* society recognizes or rewards that contribution.

So if we wanted to examine the Significance Impulse via celebrity, we would have to hone in on people who are not only famous but *also* great in that genuinely value-adding sense. Malala Yousafzai fits the bill. So does Flannery O'Connor. Martin Luther King, Jr. Albert Einstein. Ruth Bader Ginsburg. Carlos Santana. Amelia Earhart. In addition to their social recognition, these folks actually achieved a degree of importance that the private equity manager cannot claim. That is what is valued by the Significance Impulse. It says that, even if society gives you absolutely *zero* recognition or reward, it is still good for you to achieve greatness. Being great *itself* is something we should want for our lives. Ideally, according to the Significance Impulse, we should want to do something that puts us on the universe's all-time V.I.P. list, even if we already had all the money and fame in the world.

Confusing the value of importance with the value of wealth and attention is not the only way that the Impulse can get muddled. Notably, some damaged people seem to think that being extraordinary in *any* way is important, and they make their mark by hurting others. There is no doubt that we sometimes use the word "significant" in this way, to signal merely being *consequential*, regardless of whether those consequences are good or bad.[2] But for us to use the word "significant" in that way would draw us away from the impulse that drives this book. For our examination of significance, the focus will be squarely on what Ali and Williams cared about: we are only tackling the urge to be extraordinary in some *positive* way. (In case it's not yet evident, note that I am using the words "greatness," "significance," and "importance" interchangeably.)

Of course, even that qualifier is not enough, because people also get confused about what counts as positive: they mistake evil for good. Put that confusion aside, too. The impulse that we are

---

2. For example, Kahane (2022) thinks that Adolf Hitler was significant in this sense.

THE SIGNIFICANCE IMPULSE

concerned with values being *truly* important. This, as we will see, requires being a source of genuinely positive value. History's madmen, monsters, and murderers will get no attention here.[3]

Now, people who want to do something significant usually want other things, too. We want to raise a family, have a peaceful home, and enjoy a cool drink on a warm afternoon. We would like to be surrounded by beauty and to live long lives in relative comfort. Unfortunately, being significant can sometimes crowd out these other goods. Important people seem to disproportionately suffer from compromised home life, stress, addiction, social isolation, privacy incursions, death threats, and incarceration. As a 15-year-old, Malala got shot in the head. And generally speaking, important achievements can sometimes come from pursuing a passion so single-mindedly that it crowds out the benefits of a more well-rounded life. This may not be an accident; some think that single-minded focus is positively *required* for greatness.[4] It is understandable that some are alarmed that being important, and the value system that prizes importance, can have disastrous consequences for us.[5]

The question is usually thought to be how to balance these competing interests: Is it better to be significant or to have a healthier and more well-rounded life? That was Achilles' dilemma in the *Iliad*:

> If I abide here and war about the city of the Trojans, then lost is my home-return, but my renown shall be imperishable; but if I return home to my dear native land, lost then is my glorious renown, yet shall my life long endure, neither shall the doom of death come soon upon me.[6]

---

3. Except in the footnotes.

4. Hurka (1993, chap. 7); Simonton (1994).

5. Alpert (2022).

6. Homer (1924, Book 9, lines 410–415).

Achilles chose imperishable renown, but many would go the other direction and rank being significant below their other priorities. Some might want to be significant, but not so much that they would actually pursue it; and others would pursue greatness only under certain constraints, or only halfheartedly. These ways of backing away from being important nonetheless concede our starting point: to say that the downsides of significance pull you away from pursuing a more extraordinary life is to feel the Impulse tugging at you—it is to grant that being significant would be good, if we could just tame those risks.

This should compel us to ask: What if the Impulse is just entirely wrong from the start? Consider Frida Kahlo's position. After living in the United States she concluded,

> It is irritating that the most important thing for everyone in Gringolandia is to have ambition, to succeed in becoming "somebody," and frankly I no longer have even the least ambition to be anybody, I despise the conceit, and being the *gran caca* does not interest me in any way.[7]

Now, I was raised in that very same Gringolandian environment, and so I was taught to value importance just like the other residents of the self-proclaimed Greatest Country on Earth™. But I have come around to see the wisdom of the Dove, as Kahlo's parents called her: I think that, in and of itself, being important is not in our personal interests. At all. Defending that claim is the first task of this book.[8]

If this is right, then those of us who have felt the Impulse have to reexamine what we want for our very own lives: we valued being

---

7. Herrera (2002, 172).

8. Are there other ways to interpret that quote from Kahlo? Might she be talking about attention or fame more than importance? Yes, she might. But such alternative interpretations would be less useful for making my point, so naturally I must neglect them.

important, and we were mistaken to do so. But not all is lost, for this book also defends a second claim: each of us—even Ali, Kahlo, and Williams, and any other greats you might think of—just do not matter very much in the big picture. Putting these two claims together yields mixed news: we have been wrong to think that it is in our interests to be important, but that's just fine because we are fated to be unimportant anyway.

Now many people find that second thought, the one that says that we are relatively unimportant, terrifying. First, you've got your nihilists, who think that *you* don't matter because *nothing* matters. And so, they claim, we are doomed to have no reason to do or not do anything. No reason at all. I mean, why would they even say such a thing?

Then there are the pessimists, who think that things do matter, but life is awful. They trade nihilism's pile of doom for a bowl full of gloom.

And the absurdists think that our lives are a joke. Some react to that joke by stomping around about it, while others invite us to laugh at the human condition. But even for them that laughter is the most juice that we can legitimately squeeze out of the lemon of a life that we've been handed. And the price for enjoying this bit of comedy is that we get cast as the universe's hoodwinked fools.

That's a lot of dismay coming from a lot of different directions. Perhaps the most popular way to fight off the dismay is to insist that we should celebrate our place in the cosmos. We might be the center of the universe! On the religious version of this celebration, we are favored by some god; on the secular version, we are the only sources of love, rationality, agency, and consciousness in an otherwise dead and uncaring universe. Either way, this camp is confident that, if we are the only ones with such an exalted status, then our lives have tremendous significance. We are the stars of the cosmic show, the epicenter of all the value rippling through the universe, Bearers of Ultimate Worth and Big Responsibility!

Now just speaking personally, I find that role exhausting. But again, the dismal alternative seems to be that we are little more than reconstituted bug dandruff scattered across a misshapen boulder, which itself is sentenced to an eon of circling an unremarkable alleyway off a boring side street of a universe that itself matters little or not at all. All that negativity could make a person cry . . . except there's no point in crying if none of it really matters. There is no point in doing anything if none of it really matters.

All this makes it seem like we've got two choices: either optimistic glee grounded in unbridled human exceptionalism or mopey resignation that we just don't matter at all. This book aims to flesh out an option between those two poles. The possibility at the midway is that we are in fact creatures who matter . . . but only a bit. The task is to make the case that this is a happy truth. It is better to be a bit player than to have your name lit up at the top of the universe's marquee. Mattering somewhat but being relatively unimportant liberates us, we will see, to focus earnestly on the little bit of value in our world and to be more carefree about the rest. Humility about our relatively trivial existence licenses enthusiasm about the meager portion of value we get. In that space between despair and exuberance, between absurdity and pomposity, between utter pointlessness and total triumph, something wonderful awaits. There, in that boring belly of the cosmos, lies a special kind of freedom, what I will call "freedom from the tyranny of value."

So this book's thesis is that we are relatively unimportant, but that's okay, because from the perspective of self-interest, being important is overrated. Assume with me for a moment that this is true, that importance is truly not in our personal interests. In that case, your totally humdrum life is exactly as important as you should want it to be. While some people see the acknowledgment of our unimportance as a pessimistic way of looking at things, putting it in the same family as the nihilists and absurdists,[9] pessimism

---

9. For example, Kahane (2022).

requires an extra step beyond the conclusion that we do not matter very much. To get to pessimism, you would have to *also* believe that it is *good* for us to matter a lot more—a good that we miss out on if we are not very important. If instead it turns out to be better for us to be relatively unimportant, then it is not pessimistic to say that we do not matter all that much. On the contrary, it is downright upbeat. Good things, our lucky little lives. This book is an optimist's manifesto.

* * *

Think about the question of significance this way: If it were possible, would you want to be the hero who one day cures cancer?

Surely you would! You could not let all those people suffer, if it were within your power to help them. (Being honest here, you are probably a better person than I am. Unless you are one of those people who have been trying to revive 1980s fashion. Even I am not *that* bad.) Clearly you would be correct to want to see all those people spared from their suffering. But would you also be right to want *yourself* to be the one who gets to be their savior?

For the sake of focusing on importance and only importance, leave the social rewards out of it. Imagine that although you would cure cancer, you would not get noticed or applauded for it because everyone would mistakenly think that someone else cured cancer—your dastardly boss who stole your spotlight. Also, assume that if you don't discover this cure, then your rival in another lab will find the same cure a couple of days later anyway. This assumption allows us to fix on the kind of greatness that motivated Ali and Williams: they worked in competitive fields, and they wanted to be the *best*. If they fail to be the greatest in their endeavors, then someone else will take their spot. So along those same lines, would you think it is better if *you* are the one to cure cancer, even knowing that your rival will do it in your place, if you do not? Factoring out the many rewards they received, are Ali's and Williams' lives better than they would have been if they were just average professionals in their sports? Similarly, abstracting away the *costs* that Malala has had to pay for her activism, is her life improved by the fact that she paved a path for so many girls to be educated? Is Barack Obama's own well-being boosted by the fact that he was a pivotal force in bringing health care to millions of people? Was it good for John Coltrane that he changed the direction of so much music and the lives of so many music fans? Was Mary Shelley's situation better for having excavated new territory in the human imagination?

It sure seems like it. This was what the Splinter wanted, and what we tell our kids: it is good to be great. That is the Significance Impulse.

But again, this book defends the Dove's view that keeping all other things equal—factoring out the payoffs of fortune and fame, as well as the risks to health and wealth—somebodies do not live better lives than nobodies. While it is true that society often attaches external rewards to significance, and that those external rewards can be good for us, being important *itself* adds nothing of personal value to our lives. With a couple of limitations discussed in Chapters 4 and 5, this book argues that none of our personal interests are furthered by being important per se. And, more than that, we do have interests that are furthered by being *un*important. Which means, surprisingly, that you should not want to be the hero who saves humanity from cancer. Might as well leave it to that other person.

* * *

Any serious critique of the Significance Impulse must address it on its own terms. Its distinctive claim is that, *assuming* the universe has value, we should strive to be the crown jewel that shines brighter than all the rest. The assumption of value is necessary because if nothing mattered at all, then nothing would be important. So in order to meet the Impulse on its own ground, we will just *grant* to the pro-importance crowd that there is value. In other words, we assume that nihilism is false. That assumption enables us to focus on the questions of whether *we* have a lot of value and whether it is better to be someone of *more* rather than *less* value.[10]

Also assume that we humans matter in a couple of specific ways. For starters, let us grant that we are endowed with inherent moral status. We have rights, and we are entitled to a certain level and kind of consideration by others, just because of what we are as persons. Additionally, since we matter to people who themselves matter, we matter in a way that exceeds our intrinsic status: we have a secondary, derivative value sourced in our relations to others who themselves matter. One obvious example of this relational value is that you might impact many other people in some positive way. But that is only one form of relational value. Merely being the daughter of someone who matters can make the daughter matter, too. Under these assumptions, David Hume was incorrect to say that "[t]he life of man is of no greater importance to the universe than that of an oyster."[11] If anything matters (as our first assumption claims), then (second) we have more intrinsic status than an oyster, and (third) we have more relational value (like impact) than an oyster has.

So congratulations to us: we matter more than oysters! Or, at any rate, we will assume that this is so, in order to grant our pro-significance opponents their starting ground. But clearly any superiority we enjoy over oysters does not automatically elevate us to great importance in the grand scheme of things. Ali and Williams didn't just want to *matter*; they wanted to be especially *great*. This drive for greatness (as contrasted now with merely mattering) is what this book is putting on trial, so it is safe to assume that we are *somewhat* significant in the more modest sense of mattering *at all*. The more *im*modest sense of extraordinary significance is what is at stake between Williams and Kahlo, and it is what people hope for when in thrall to the Significance Impulse. Whether we might

---

10. Kahane (2014). We briefly return to examine some nihilistic themes in Chapter 6.

11. Hume (1777).

be important in that *extraordinary* sense, and whether that would be good for us, is the question with which our book starts, and so as we pursue that question we are safe in assuming that we matter *somewhat*.

Eventually the evidence will show that even under the assumption that we matter in these ways, still we are not especially significant in the biggest picture. What is more, we all matter almost exactly the same amount as each other, because almost all of what matters in us—our humanity, our consciousness, our cares, our pleasures and pains, our relationships, our projects, our pursuits—are things we have in roughly equal shares. The big shots do have a *bit* more of what matters, because they have outsize impact. But on a cosmic scale, that surplus adds only a fraction of value more than what all of us have to begin with. And that ain't much.

* * *

One person very important to American legal circles in the 1900s, Judge Learned Hand, once imagined what a first day in heaven would look like for him.[12] He said that it would begin with him being the most important player in a baseball game, and then in a football game. In the evening he would attend a banquet with all of history's greatest figures. We can excuse the hubris: Judge Hand was merely following a long tradition of important people wanting to eat with other important people.

As the evening progresses in Hand's divine fantasy, one of the greatest wordsmiths of all time, Voltaire, gets up to give a speech at this Supper of the Stars. But then, in an unexpected twist, the crowd shouts down Voltaire. They want Judge Hand to speak instead! In Hand's heaven, he is the most important person in history in the endeavors he cares about—putting words together and playing the two sports most popular in twentieth-century America.

12. Garvey (2011, 27).

If the argument laid out in the rest of this book is right, then Hand, like Ali, Williams, and so many others, is basking in a false dream. What heaven looks like is not *you* doing the important thing, but rather the important thing *happening*. Writing about all the misery in the world, Iddo Landau puts the key point nicely: "my desire is for the suffering to stop, not that I should affect those who suffer. If the suffering ended in the right way at the hands of other agents . . . I would be just as content."[13] He and I are on the same Kahloesque page. Just. As. Content. Once we leave aside the contingent external rewards that society attaches to doing the valuable deed, it does not matter who does the valuable deed. What matters is only that the valuable deed gets done. It does not matter who rescues sufferers from their suffering, as long as someone does. And it does not matter who gives the after-dinner speech, as long as it is entertaining.

We are right to want whatever matters in the world—peace, happiness, health, love, tacos. These things are good. Noticing this, we then think, again rightly, that we have reason to make the world a better place by making those good things a reality. Cure cancer (or become a nurse). Unify physics (or teach teenagers science). End racism (or agitate for equality in your local community). Stabilize the climate (or avoid single-use plastic). But we then go a further step, and it is one step too far. We conflate value per se with value *that accrues to the one who creates value*. This, I think, is what the Dove saw. She understood that what we have *some* reason to do gets easily conflated with what we have reasons of *self-interest specifically* to do. The young person thinks not just that the climate needs to be stabilized but that their life will be amazing if they are the one who stabilizes the climate. Or that it is in their interests to be the one who cures cancer. The thought is that these are lives worth striving for, *even if somebody else instead of you would do the exact same important works*. This step, from the idea that important things should

13. Landau (2017, 99).

THE SPLINTER AND THE DOVE   *13*

happen to the distinct idea that it is in our own personal interests to be the ones to make them happen, is the error at the heart of the Significance Impulse. We seem to think that if we do what is valuable, some of that value will rub off on our own lives. But it doesn't.

That will seem to many like bad news: any value we put into the world does not necessarily improve the value we get to enjoy in our *own* lives. But the good news, remember, is that being insignificant is just fine: it does not make your life worse if you don't matter very much. In fact, we will see some ways in which being unimportant is actually in your interests.

Welcome to a celebration of being ordinary.

2
Value Rare and High

What does it mean to call something "significant" or "important," in the sense that concerns us?

In one perfectly normal use of the term "important," doing something of importance is tantamount to doing something of *value*.[1] And merely doing something of value does make us significant in the sense of not being *totally insignificant*, or of *merely mattering somewhat*. But, as we saw in Chapter 1, this sense of "significance" or "importance" is not the relevant one for us. While there is value in us crocheting, playing soccer, and baking bread, these minor feats do not call others to turn their gaze upon us— they are not important in the grander sense presupposed by the Significance Impulse.[2] The value obtained in knitting a sweater does not give me the level of importance that distinguishes the historical Buddha, Siddhartha Gautama, from your Average Joe—the kind of significance at issue between Kahlo and Williams. What we are asking, in this book, is: What is the difference between the ordinary

---

1. Smith (2006).

2. Harrison (1978, 221); Kahane (2014, 2022).

The Significance Impulse. Joshua Glasgow, Oxford University Press. © Oxford University Press 2024.
DOI: 10.1093/9780197754788.003.0002

and the extraordinary? What separates a pretty good hitter from the greatest hitter of all time?

Among other things, only one person can be the greatest hitter who ever lived. What the Splinter and the Dove were onto is the question of whether it is good to be *exceptional*. Vindicating the Impulse requires showing that it is good to matter in some extraordinary way like this. Among other things, this means that in the relevant sense, to be important in some endeavor is to be relatively *rare* in that endeavor.[3]

The rarity requirement straightaway means that you and I are probably not especially significant. Or even if you are rare in some respect and so important in that respect—Your son's only mother! The peninsula's greatest arranger of dominos!—still you are probably not important in most other respects. We talk (implicitly or explicitly) in such a way that how rare, and so how significant, you are depends on both what you are compared to (the peninsula or the entire world?) and what the relevant standards of evaluation are (arranging dominos or ending global poverty?). I will refer to these two parameters jointly as "context."

While restricted contexts are often implied in judgments of importance, we can also remove both parameters and ascend to a megacontext where one supreme standard of evaluation determines overall importance compared to everything that exists. Some religious people, for example, believe that, considering every value in the universe, their god is the most important thing of all. Let us follow tradition and call this absolute context the "cosmic" scale.

The existence of cosmic importance is compatible with there being a more limited "Did you change pop music?" or a "How much do you matter in Peoria?" scale of significance, too. Consequently, we've got one recipe for being important that we can always whip up for ourselves: just define the contextual parameters in a way that shines a light on your distinctive strengths, and you will have

---

3. James (2015, 327); Kahane (2014); Smilansky (2012, 120).

guaranteed your rarity and importance within that context. After all, it is a lot easier to be the greatest *author of this book* (that's me!) than it is to be the greatest *thing in the universe* (probably not me). And as Thomas Nagel points out, a certain kind of value attaches to things just by virtue of their *particularity*.[4] So can't we each be equally important just by being rare in our own unique way?

Well, no. Nagel reminds us that a ketchup bottle has its particularity, too. Behold its glorious redness and glassness and hereness and nowness! This is not what people seek when they act on the Significance Impulse. Any value in mere particularity is not the kind of importance that this book is focused on—the sense in which the Buddha was more important than the equally particular (if average) Average Joe, the kind of importance that Williams celebrates and Kahlo repudiates. Like merely being of value, merely being rare does not call for the world's attention. So, if everything is rare in its own way, and if that is not enough to make everything important in the sense that is relevant to our discussion, then some other element, besides rarity and merely being of value, must also help determine significance.

The missing element is that the important thing needs to have relatively *high* value.[5] The sense of significance that concerns us—the goal that Ted Williams embraced before ensuring that his postmortem head would be immersed for ultralong storage in liquid nitrogen—contrasts both with being *ordinary* and with being *trivial*. It is what we are talking about when we say that the problem of kids going hungry is important, while a celebrity's (trivial) dating life is not so important, and that curing cancer is important, while eating an (ordinary) cantaloupe is not. Relative to context—that is, against a given contrast class and measured by some operative standard of evaluation—things that are important in our sense don't just matter; they matter *a lot*. As the parameters get more general,

---

4. Nagel (1986, 222–223).

5. Cf. Nozick (1989, 173); Singer (1992, 114).

covering more instances and/or more evaluated properties, the bar of what counts as sufficiently high value gets raised.

So these are the crucial ingredients for significance in the rel-, evant sense: significant or important things are both rare and of high value, relative to a context. Notice that if this is what it takes to be important, then we can explain how importance comes in *degrees*. Other things being equal, the higher the value you produce (or instantiate), the more important you are; and, again other things equal, the rarer you are with respect to that value, the more important you are.

* * *

Our next question, then, is obvious: How might we get our hands on some of that relatively high and rare value?

Perched on a balcony in Vienna, William James thought he found an answer. Finding himself moved by the sight of some peasants below, he concluded that importance lies in the routine, the plain, the humble. Our public monuments should be dedicated "[n]ot to our generals and poets," he wrote, turning Horace in his grave, "but to the Italian and Hungarian laborers in the Subway."[6] For James, those people worthy of veneration have some sort of virtue, such as being a hard worker, motivated by an "ideal" within them. To be sure, the toil alone is not enough. Nor is it enough just to believe in some values. ("Your college professor, with a starched shirt and spectacles, would, if a stock of ideals were all alone by itself enough to render a life significant, be the most absolutely and deeply significant. . .") You need both, James held: the significant life is a life where a dream drives the toil. If you let your ideal guide your virtue into action, your "inner joy, courage, and endurance" will express themselves and change the world.[7] The worker, the artist, the scientist whose labor is driven by the goal of making the

6. James (1899, 62–63).

7. James (1899, 83, 82).

world a better place: they are the ones we ought to glorify, because they are the ones who are truly important.

Though James did not say this, surely that stew of industry and ideals should get results, too. One way we judge which efforts are important is based on their outcomes.[8] In particular, the more that something has a valuable impact on valuable creatures, the more significant it is; some think that impact is even *essential* to being important.[9]

Now you might question whether our impact is really able to make us important, since whatever impact we make, someone else might have made that impact instead. That is Nagel's basis for saying that our existence is "entirely gratuitous": although the world might be better for having *people* in it, there is unlikely to be added value in having the *particular* people it has. If different people had been here instead of us, the world would have had roughly the same value that the actual world has. According to this line of thought, if I hadn't taught my students, somebody else would have, so I cannot be very important.[10]

Nagel concedes that it might have been a "real loss" if we hadn't gotten Mozart or Einstein. By altering the trajectory of history, big names like them do make an "irreplaceable difference" that some take to be the key to importance.[11] Consider what distinguishes Alexander Fleming from whoever cleaned his lab. The story of Fleming's discovery of penicillin is that, while away from his lab for a couple of weeks, he left out a petri dish that contained staphylococcus bacteria. The petri dish was neither stored as planned nor cleaned up by any staff. When he returned to the lab, Fleming noticed that the staphylococcus was stifled by the penicillin

---

8. Nozick (1981, 582); Nozick (1989, chap. 16); Singer (1992, 117).

9. Frankfurt (1999, 85).

10. Nagel (1986, 213).

11. Levy (2005, 186 n. 22).

that had accidentally contaminated the petri dish in his absence. Because it took his keen eye to catch that, it seems like, if Fleming hadn't existed, penicillin would not have been discovered when it was; whereas if a different person had been in charge of straightening up Fleming's lab, then assuming that other person followed the same practice of leaving Fleming's petri dishes untouched, we still would have gotten penicillin when we did. Fleming was irreplaceable in the discovery of penicillin, while his lab cleaner was replaceable. Nagel's view is effectively that in the workplace of life, most of us are the janitor. If we had not existed, the world's total value would not have changed very much. But maybe at least a couple of folks like Fleming can get the rare and high value of importance by doing something nobody else would have done.

As understandable as that line of thought may be, I think it is mistaken. To say this is not to say that, in reality, each of us makes an irreplaceable contribution to the world. Rather, it is to say that being replaceable is not relevant to the value of a person's impact. As David Benatar puts it: "Even if somebody else would have discovered penicillin when [Fleming] did, the fact remains that *he* discovered it. He made the difference."[12] Being the actual discoverer is a way in which Fleming made an important difference, even if somebody else would have discovered penicillin if he hadn't—even if he was as replaceable as the custodian. Some good we contribute to the world can increase our value, and thus our importance, even if our contribution would have been made by someone else had we not made it.

Consider an analogy. If you hadn't fallen in love with your partner, you probably would have fallen in love with somebody else awhile later. Call it the Tinder Principle: the value we get from our loves is replaceable. Notably, that does not make your actual partner less important in your life. Importance seems to hang not on *irre-*

---

12. Benatar (2017, 31; emphasis in original); cf. Smuts (2013). For further discussion, and disagreement, see also Bramble (2015, 450–451); Kauppinen (2012, sec. 4).

placeably contributing value but more simply on *actually* contributing value. You just have to make a difference, even if someone else could or even would have made that same difference, to produce some value in the world.[13]

To apply that lesson more broadly, reflect on Isaac Newton and Gottfried Wilhelm Leibniz, widely hailed as two of humanity's most important thinkers. While they started out as polite colleagues, corresponding briefly across the English Channel, their relationship would eventually descend into an acrid dispute that one observer has called "the greatest intellectual property debate of all time."[14] The stakes were high not just because of their historic levels of petty jerkiness; they were also fighting over credit for one of their greatest creations: Who was the first to invent calculus? (Let me spoil it for you. Ignoring some historical antecedents, Newton came up with it first but didn't publish it right away; Leibniz independently invented it later and then published it before Newton.) Brightening history's unflattering glare on this Grade A beef is the fact that math and science were inevitably marching toward this discovery of calculus anyway: by the time Leibniz and Newton got on the project, "[a]ll the basic work was done—somebody just needed to take the next step and put it all together. If Newton and Leibniz had not discovered it, someone else would have."[15] So if Newton would have never given the world calculus, Leibniz did anyway. And if Leibniz had not given the world calculus, Newton would have. And if neither one of them did the job, some third person would have.

---

13. Although some people fear that their lovers might "move on" after losing them (Moller 2007, esp. 309–310), the fact of the matter is that we *can* find other loves, which confirms that the sense in which we are and want to be important to those we love is not by being more important than any alternative love might have been but simply by being of uniquely high *actual* value to them. On this front, I am sympathetic to the theory that actual history, rather than appealing intrinsic qualities, is what grounds love (Grau 2006, 2010; Kolodny 2003; Abramson and Leite 2011).

14. Bardi (2006, viii).

15. Bardi (2006, 29).

For both of them it was true that the world would have had calculus, around the same time, even without their contribution. And yet, crucially, we do not think that this diminishes their importance.

All this confirms that to be important, what you have to do is actually create rare and high value. That's it. In particular, you can have the kind of rare and high value that makes you extraordinarily important even if someone else would have had the same rare and high value if you hadn't existed—even if, à la Newton and Leibniz, someone else *does* have the same value that you have. In the small context of my university during my time, I can be important to my students even if, in my absence, someone else would have taught them just as well as I did. Actual impact is one way to be important, regardless of replaceability.

At the same time, having a broad impact on others (replaceable or not) is not the only way to get the high value of significance. In his recollection of life at Auschwitz, Viktor Frankl observed how a false hierarchy imposed by the Nazi guards was internalized:

> The majority of prisoners suffered from a kind of inferiority complex. We all had once been or had fancied ourselves to be "somebody." Now we were treated like complete nonentities. . . . Without consciously thinking about it, the average prisoner felt himself utterly degraded.[16]

In Frankl's estimation, the people who exhibited true "human greatness" amid that awful degradation were those who found strength when others gave up, a purpose that they could fulfill when others found only despair.[17] This suggests that even when significance does hinge on impact, the relevant impact is not always about affecting others; sometimes it is about impacting one's own self. We might say the same thing about a rarely achieved level of Buddhist

16. Frankl (1959, 61).

17. Frankl (1959, 71–80, 115).

enlightenment or excellence in a relatively obscure sport: people who scale such heights have done something important despite the fact that they haven't impacted huge numbers of other people in any extraordinary way. Just consider the examples of Paige Pierce or Paul McBeth.[18]

More than that, the outcome of one's efforts might generate the high value of importance without positively impacting *anyone*, including even oneself. Perhaps Coltrane's most stunning playing happened during a solitary practice session that he was not personally moved by. Maybe the most beautiful painting ever created is squirreled away in a closet, unseen. Being hidden from the public, such works of art would lack any cultural sway. What is more, sometimes artistic creations actually *harm* their creators, such as by evoking overwhelmingly traumatic memories. In a case like that, despite the overall lack of positive impact, such artworks still have high and rare value. They are still important. This is exactly why we try to find lost art. To paraphrase Plato, a newly found piece of art does not gain its import when it finally impacts an audience; instead, it had its import all along, and that is why it rightly impacts an audience. In this way, a lack of internal or external positive impact does not diminish importance.

If all of this is right, then because there are many ways of being valuable, there are many ways to be important: you can get significance from your impact on others or yourself, or from what you are, or from what you create (impactful or not), or from merely mattering to others. Each of these different sites can hold value in greater or lesser amounts and be more or less rare. So, they are where we can search for our importance: *Do we have that sort of rare and high value?* As we see next, the most complete answer to this question is that in the cosmic context, even the most valuable among us are not very important. Not even Paige Pierce and Paul McBeth.

---

18. *Who are they?* you ask. And I answer: *Exactly.*

3

The Sage's Argument

We saw in the previous chapter that you might be important in some contextualized ways. You matter to your friends. You are really important in the world of archery. You are a community leader. The question of our *cosmic* significance removes these parameters. It asks how we stack up, not against other students or chefs or labor organizers but against *everything, everywhere, for all time, by all standards*. We climb past the timberline, scale up above mountain ranges, pull away from the sun and its planets, and zoom out so far that galaxies become pointillistic eddies. This scope is almost contemptuous of stars and their little satellites like Earth. The cosmic context is the context that cannot be exceeded; its range is all.

How should we evaluate our import through that lens? Famously, the innumerable stars, the universe's immeasurable distances, incomprehensible age, and overwhelming forces, and the sheer enormity of everything that exists all diminish us, as a mountain towering beside an ant's egg. Our time is an imperceptible ping on the ancient arc of the cosmos, our burn barely a flicker in the shimmering night sky. We take up a thimbleful of room and only weakly tug on the loosest threads in the tapestry of the firmament. We little clumps propel around for a few moments, and then we

The Significance Impulse. Joshua Glasgow, Oxford University Press. © Oxford University Press 2024.
DOI: 10.1093/9780197754788.003.0003

decompose. Thus the sages, poets, cosmologists, and teenagers have widely agreed: we are cosmically insignificant.[1]

So sure, you might be able to control some of what happens in your workplace. But even the titans of industry are not capable of making much of a difference cosmically speaking. You might live more than a century, and that will turn out to be just this side of nothing in a universe that is billions of years old and marching toward who knows how many billions more. You could potentially undertake a gargantuan construction project, erecting a skyscraper perhaps. From a perspective that includes solar storms and supernovas, that's merely a scratch on a tiny surface. As we adopt the cosmic scale, it quickly becomes clear that even the most important among us—the world leaders, history-making artists, and celebrated heroes—are very limited in the power to do much of anything.

Sitting here tucked away in our tiny corner of the cosmos, could we push back against the sage's argument? Is there a way to defend our importance? One option is to reject the whole project of assessing cosmic significance. Alternatively, we could challenge the idea that qualities like power, size, and duration are genuinely relevant to measuring how significant we are. Finally, one might want to say that there are *other* qualities, besides size, power, or duration, that *do* matter a lot, and which we happen to have in ample amounts.

Can any of these replies work?

* * *

Let us start with challenges to the very project of determining our cosmic significance. Given our earthbound existence and distinctively human concerns, why should we care about the rest of the universe? Why is the cosmic scale relevant for evaluating our lives?

---

1. See, for example, Russell (2008).

Now perhaps what ultimately *matters most* is something earthly.[2] What I take to be the best interpretation of that point is that the cosmic scale does not affect the things we care most about and should most want for ourselves, such as living a good and meaningful life. But even if cosmic considerations do not impact life's most important values (and I will add fuel to that fire in Chapters 4 and 5), this point does not make the cosmic scale irrelevant to determining our importance. It does not affect the sage's argument that our tiny size, short lives, and profound weakness do in fact make us cosmically insignificant. Rather, it affects the next step where being cosmically insignificant is taken to be grounds for pessimism about our lot in life. We will return to that pessimism soon. For now our focus is on the preceding question of whether we *are* important, leaving until later the investigation of whether being unimportant affects what matters for our lives.

Another way of diminishing the cosmic perspective is to insist that for something to matter, it must matter *to someone*. In that case, unless we presuppose the existence of a cosmic-sized god, then there would be no cosmic-level perspective from which our cosmic import is determined. The idea of a cosmic perspective might even look to some people like the lingering stain of a more superstitious time, when it made sense to imagine that the universe itself evaluates us and everything else it contains.[3] We know better now.

Talk of the "cosmic perspective" is shorthand for a *scale*, or for a *scope* of evaluation. It is not literally a point of view, as if the cosmos were alive and examining its insides. It requires no god—though it is compatible with all gods. In fact, despite the turn of phrase, the cosmic perspective requires no distinctive *perspective* at all, literally

---

2. Landau (2017, 98–100; cf. Landau 2011). For other rejections of the cosmic perspective, see Belliotti (2001, 56; cf. 81); Gordon (1984, 26); Jollimore (2020); Persson and Savulescu (2019, 235).

3. Williams (2006, 137). See also Blackburn (2001, 89–90); Hare (1972, 34–35); Korsgaard (2018, esp. 9–12).

speaking. Cosmic evaluations take up a totally normal point of view and simply adjust its *range*: they examine our own value compared with everything, as opposed to comparing us with smaller contrast classes (like each other or world history, for example).[4]

The question of which scope we want to adopt is separate from the question of what perspective we must take when evaluating what matters within that given scope. My brother matters more to me than your brother matters to me, and your brother matters to you more than mine does. But whether we look at how someone matters from my perspective or from yours, or perhaps from an impartial perspective, there is also the clearly separate question of them mattering on a local scale or on a regional or global-historical or galactic or cosmic scale. My brother is very important from my perspective, but even within that perspective I still realize that he has little global-historical import. In the sage's argument what has our significance on the run is this rapidly expanding *range*, not some mysterious eye that sees and judges all.

So cosmic significance does not require some inscrutable point of view held in the mind of an intergalactic monster. To say that we are cosmically unimportant is just to say that, relative to literally everything and accounting for literally every value, we do not matter very much. This claim is unthreatened by the idea that perspectives need to be human, since it can be made within the human perspective. The cosmic scale is just a scale. It is only one scale among many. That makes it neither suspect nor inhuman.

A hardliner about this sort of thing could retreat to a relativist approach where something matters exactly as much as you *think* it matters. In that case, if you think you have cosmic importance, then relative to you, truly you are that significant. And sure enough, if you are this kind of relativist, then we have to part ways. For if mattering is radically relative in that way, then there is no point in talking about importance at all. Instead, the answer to the question

4. Kahane (2014, 750).

of importance would be baked right into the relativism: everyone is exactly as important as they think they are. That is not how our question works. Such relativists could not, for example, join Ali, Williams, and other sports fans in debating who the greatest is. The radical relativist thinks that such disagreements make no sense: if you are just as great as you think you are, end of story, then there is no point disagreeing about who the greatest is. By contrast, to examine the Impulse on its merits, we must proceed on the assumption that there are non-relative truths about how much things matter. Our project commits us to non-relativistic assessments of importance.

Beyond the fact that radical relativism is irrelevant to the debate between defenders and opponents of the Significance Impulse, it also appears to be false. It has a difficult time making sense of the idea that we sometimes have our priorities out of whack. Radical relativists have to say that the only mistakes that we can make about what is important are those in which we misread our own minds—where we didn't know what we ourselves really deemed important. But some mistakes, especially some of our most regrettable mistakes, happen when we read our minds correctly and only later discover that our minds came, genuinely and authentically, to flawed judgments about what really matters. That is, whether and how, and how much, something *actually* matters seem to be determined outside of our individual judgments. The bare possibility that our judgments about what is important can be mistaken means that the truth of those judgments must be grounded on *something* outside of the attitudes of the person making the mistake. That is incompatible with radical relativism.

The standards that govern non-relative value judgments like these might be objective in a robust sense: perhaps values decide the correctness of our judgments of importance independently of anybody recognizing those values—the values lie out there in the things themselves, as it were. But it is also possible that the objectivity we seek might be internal to us in certain ways. Perhaps the objectivity is something as human as the value projected onto the world by collective agreement, or maybe objectivity derives from idealized versions of our attitudes. So long as those standards remain outside of the evaluation in question, they are sufficiently "objective" for our purposes.[5] We just have to believe that we can make mistakes in our valuations, mistakes that might exceed what we want or prefer or affirm or approve in any given moment of choice. Those who are tempted by some kind of relativism can construe the non-relativity of the governing evaluative standards in that more minimal kind of way and still track with our project.

Obviously, it is hard for us to know what does and does not have objective value. You think that spending a couple of hours each day just picking up objects and putting them back down is a stupid waste of time. But then a quick trip to the gym introduces you to some weightlifters who disagree.[6] How do we decide which evaluation is right? The only way out of this epistemic predicament is to try to render coherent our most complete and careful judgments of what is, and what is not, objectively valuable. This is an imperfect, fallible project. But our trouble in determining which priorities are soundest is not itself a reason to reject the idea of objective value. After all, we don't reject the facts of science just because we sometimes have a hard time figuring them out.

With a commitment to objective value, then, return to the sage's argument. To be a local hero, you don't need to jump from planet to planet, saving lives as you go. But you cannot be a *cosmic* hero unless you can manage interstellar leaps. Compared to the bruise, the broken arm is significant; but compared to the tumor, it is not. Similarly, compared to the clump of dirt, you are powerful; but compared to a black hole, you are not. To recognize different contexts of comparison is to concede the point: in the cosmic context, we are lacking.

A different argument for undermining the very question of cosmic significance is that a specifically human, not cosmic, perspective

---

5. Calhoun (2018, 21); Levy (2005, 180); Fischer (2020, 13); Wolf (2010b).

6. Cahn (2008, 237).

is baked into our value judgments by virtue of their being shaped by natural selection.[7] But notice that, first, the cosmic perspective is plausibly integrated with a highly functional (and hence potentially selected-for) capacity. It is just one instance of a more general ability to evaluate things at different levels of generality—the ability to expand and shrink the context within which we compare and rank options. We can evaluate how important we are relative to our co-workers; we wonder about how we stack up in our communities; and then we can investigate how important we are on a global scale, or even a historical scale. At each level, we ascend to a wider scope of evaluation. The cosmic scope is just the widest perspective, the last ascension, the point at which we ask how important we are compared to *everything*. Arguably, this ability to expand and shrink our scopes of evaluation is advantageous: it helps us think through a very wide range of problems, including those that our early ancestors faced, from getting a needed meal to protecting their children from the elements to figuring out how to organize their proto-societies. If our ancestors had not been able to make evaluations that covered various ranges of comparison, it is hard to imagine how they and their offspring would have lasted long enough to eventually produce us. I mean, would you mate with a caveperson who couldn't tell the difference between enough food to feed themselves and enough food to feed a whole family? Scope matters.

In addition, it is unclear why, even if natural selection somehow did favor merely earthly-scale evaluations, that would undermine the relevance of cosmic evaluations.[8] We want to know what has rare and high value at a variety of scales. That question floats free of whatever attitudes natural selection might or might not favor.

7. Metz (2013, 245).

8. Notice that this is a different point than one that uses evolutionary considerations to cast doubt on the whole reality of value (Street 2006). Our question here is about whether evolutionary considerations make certain scales irrelevant to value *given* that value is real in some sense (a given that was established in concession to the Significance Impulse).

The relevant ranges of value need not be constrained by what we happen to have thought about value. Perhaps there is some tendon that can connect the inert bone of evolutionarily shaped attitudes to this active muscle of value's scale, but it is not clear what that is.

Changing scale—changing context—will change our evaluation. I may matter very little to the world at large but matter a lot to my close social network. So when the sage insists that we are cosmically insignificant, we can rightfully remind them that we are still significant to our loved ones and our immediate communities. But by that same reasoning, the sage can also remind us that there is a lot more to the cosmos besides our own little networks of value. There is a whole universe out there, and for it we matter very little.

* * *

If there is no reason to reject on principle the very project of cosmic evaluation, then we can turn our attention to the two other responses to the sage's argument—responses that compete with it on its home court, as it were, rather than insisting that the cosmic field is not worth playing on. One of these two responses maintains that size, duration, and power are irrelevant to value. If that is correct, then our cosmic minuteness is irrelevant to our importance. The other response is to show that we have a cosmically generous supply of some other qualities that *do* impact importance.

Frank Ramsey was a fan of both responses: "The stars may be large," he writes, "but they cannot think or love; and these are qualities which impress me far more than size does. I take no credit for weighing nearly seventeen stone." And thinking and loving may not be the only alternative generators of significance. Riding in Ramsey's wake, Guy Kahane argues that if we and our planet's other critters hold the only sentience in the universe, and if sentience is what generates value, then Earth's sentient creatures would be the only intrinsically valuable things in the universe. If having intrinsic value is the sun around which significance orbits, we would be the source of all the significance there is. We could be the most

THE SAGE'S ARGUMENT   *31*

significant thing in the entire cosmos![9] So we must examine both conjectures: first, that our paltry size, duration, and power don't affect our significance; and second, that our plentiful sentience, lovingness, rationality, or agency do make us significant. At least, they make us significant if it turns out that we are the only things with these traits in an otherwise cold and dead universe—if we are rare in having this value.

Ordinary ways of talking about what is significant seem to entail that size, duration, and power can impact how important something is. (And note that these ordinary thoughts occur within our normal human perspective, for what that's worth.) But some believe that for something to be valuable it has to do more than that: it must impact somebody or some creature who can be benefited. To whatever extent size or age or power is importance-generating, it is only because *we care about* or *are affected by* those things, on that way of looking at the issue. *We* (and other creatures sufficiently like us) are what ultimately matters because we can fare well or poorly. Everything *else* matters only insofar as it affects welfare-capable subjects like us. This is "welfarism."

There are various ways of interpreting the welfarist claim. Anthropocentrists say specifically that if something doesn't impact *human* life, then it cannot have value. A more inclusive view holds that if something doesn't impact any *creatures capable of suffering*, then it cannot have value. A third version says that to be valuable is to make a difference to *rational* nature. But however we spell out the details (and there are others, too, such as those that single out *consciousness* or *agency*), the key welfarist move is to insist that in and of themselves size, duration, and power have no relevance to value, and so no relevance to importance; instead, these qualities are only relevant insofar as they affect what *does* have value, namely welfare-enabled creatures like us. Ben Bramble articulates the welfarist instinct this way: "What is the point of making beauti-

---

9. Ramsey (1931, 291); Kahane (2014, 2022). See also Hughes (2017); Trisel (2019).

32 THE SIGNIFICANCE IMPULSE

ful objects, gaining knowledge of the world, or developing skills, if nobody—not even oneself—will benefit from these things? Intuitively, it would be better to confer even the smallest benefit upon somebody than to do any of these things."[10]

Now it might be *better* to benefit a person than to create beauty that nobody ever enjoys. But even if that is true, we should resist the view that for something to simply have *any* value it must affect some creature's well-being: even if an ugly thing that impacts human interests is more important than a beautiful thing that impacts nobody, still, I think, beauty has value on its own, and therefore its own ability to be a site of significance. To be clear about what this claim amounts to, we might allow that ecosystems and wind and distant uninhabited planets have no *moral* status if they don't affect creatures like us. This is sometimes contested, but put that debate aside. What is easier to challenge is the idea that only welfare-affecting things have value of *any* kind. That is, while we might debate whether it is *morally* wrong for the last person alive to cut down all the trees,[11] the prospects are not nearly as strong for the welfarist claim that the universe loses no value *at all* if all the trees are cut down by the last human.

Perhaps this alternative, anti-welfarist position can be seen most charitably in cases of creative types like Dickinson and Kafka, who apparently were uninterested in seeing their writings published. Artists sometimes feel compelled to create new art even though they know that neither they nor some audience will get any benefit from it. Even if the tortured artist was made *miserable* by creating the art

---

10. Bramble (2015, 458); cf. Kahane (2014, 757–758). One move in this debate distinguishes between two kinds of significance: something that impacts the gravitational pull of a star in a remote part of the universe, for example, has *causal* significance but not necessarily *value* significance; it has impact on something even if that impact doesn't change the total value in the cosmos (Hughes 2017). Though these two different uses of "significance" are common, we still need to figure out if welfarism is true—if something must affect the welfare of a creature in order to be significant in the value-laden sense that is our concern (Kahane 2022).

11. Routley (1973); Rolston (1975). For more on how welfarist questions play out in environmental ethics, see, for example, Grey (1993).

and will bury it once it is created, there is a value in it. Consider the Library at Alexandria being destroyed: to channel Plato again, we cannot account for all its lost value merely on the grounds that some people were affected by the loss; additionally, people were affected by the loss because there was value *there* that was lost. I thus stand with G. E. Moore on this one:

> Let us imagine one world exceedingly beautiful. Imagine it as beautiful as you can; put into it whatever on this earth you most admire—mountains, rivers, the sea; trees, and sunsets, stars and moon. Imagine these all combined in the most exquisite proportions, so that no one thing jars against another, but each contributes to increase the beauty of the whole. And then imagine the ugliest world you can possibly conceive. Imagine it simply one heap of filth, containing everything that is most disgusting to us, for whatever reason, and the whole, as far as may be, without one redeeming feature.... The only thing we are not entitled to imagine is that any human being ever has or ever, by any possibility, *can*, live in either, can ever see and enjoy the beauty of the one or hate the foulness of the other. Well, even so, supposing them quite apart from any possible contemplation by human beings; still, is it irrational to hold that it is better that the beautiful world should exist, than the one which is ugly?[12]

Though some disagree, the intuitive answer to Moore's question seems to be that it is better for an otherwise inconsequential beautiful world to be created than for an otherwise inconsequential ugly world to be created.[13] But the rejection of welfarism does raise a follow-up question: What could make the Taj Mahal potentially significant, while a clump of dirt is not, if not because the clump affects nobody while the Taj Mahal moves us? Once we say that

12. Moore (1903, chap. 3, sec. 50).

13. Some simply deny this intuition. Others offer arguments against his position. Bramble (2014) holds that our collective existence is valuable only if there is some unseen order in

34   THE SIGNIFICANCE IMPULSE

value can be found in a universe devoid of creatures who can fare well or poorly, the next question asks which qualities of valuable things make them valuable. What difference between a neon light-bulb and the Pillars of Creation explains why the latter is important while the former is not?

This is where size, age, power, and beauty seem to provide good answers. Start with size: the universe's biggest object is significant, even if it never impacts any sentient creature in any way. Why do people visit the Grand Canyon and not some more medium-sized canyon? At least in part, it's because of size (as well as beauty, which some mid-sized canyons also display—and we visit those, too, of course). You can read articles about Giant Rock, but I doubt you'll find any about Regular Rock.[14] Even if your neighbor found a small but exact—and very unlikely—duplicate of the Grand Canyon hidden deep in her tangled mess of a property, you'd still care more about the Grand Canyon, *just because it's so damn big*.

Similarly, we find distinctive value in the old and long-lasting, not only in the worn walls of the Grand Canyon but also in the planet's oldest tree or a primordial meteorite from the farthest reaches of the universe; these things have value due to their age. Carolyn Korsmeyer explains that this is why it is a thrill to stand in a dinosaur footprint, and human artifacts work the same way, too: an ancient vase that is broken and otherwise quite plain matters more than a contemporary functional and beautiful vase, merely

---

which some other being or beings can benefit from us. This strikes me as a *reductio* of welfarism. Instead, I see final value as simply being a part of a better rather than worse world (Bradley 2006). See also Wolf (2010a) for a different rejection of Moore's isolation test. Wolf's view is semi-welfarist to the extent that she says value requires the *ability* to impact our experience, even if no one *actually* experiences the value (p. 59). We can, I think, take the next step and hold that if something's good-making features are good-making even without the observer actually experiencing them, then they are good-making even in the absence of any observer. For more skepticism about Moore's test and embrace of some sort of welfarism, see, for example, Belshaw (2005, 112); Blackburn (2001, 79–80); Chappell (2007, 34); Kahane (2014); Nagel (1971, 717). For another welfarist about importance specifically, see Harrison (1978).

14. Marek (2021).

because it is really old. Old things, both natural and cultural, have "age value."[15]

On this way of thinking, size and duration carry value, which means that they can determine significance. Even the world's largest ball of twine has a wee skosh of significance, despite its ridiculousness. It lacks the history, the power, and the beauty of the Grand Canyon; but still, we judge size worth caring about: some people might travel to visit the world's largest ball of twine, but nobody travels to visit a regular-sized ball of twine. More commonly, we expend great resources to see the giant redwoods, not ordinary Douglas firs, because the giants are giant. And old. Their size and age make them rare and valuable—significant sights to see.

In this light it almost seems that the only way to reject the significance of size is if you have not walked a crease in the Alps or the Himalayas; that those who question the value of old age seem to have never been thrilled by chiseling a prehistoric fossil from caked dirt; that those who dismiss power have not been cowed by the Pacific Ocean's might during king tides and a fierce winter storm. Many of us are taught to find our sense of awe and cherish these things. What could that valuation be grounded on, if size, power, and duration have no value to ground how we should feel?[16] Awe, wonder, and similar attitudes seem to be rational reactions to size, power, and duration that take the form of value judgments.[17] The only way to preserve this web of normative relations is to recognize that those quantitative properties can ground value.

But does having old things really make for a better world? James Lenman questions whether it makes things better if, say, white rhi-

15. Korsmeyer (2008; 2016, 226; 2019, esp. 79–85).

16. Thus one influential account of awe maintains that *vastness* is one central component of awe (Keltner and Haidt 2003). See also Kristjánsson (2017, 131–133); McShane (2018, 473–474).

17. For an extended, comprehensive examination and defense of this claim, see Coates (2022).

36 THE SIGNIFICANCE IMPULSE

nos are around for five billion as opposed to five million years.[18] And this makes sense in one respect: if we are looking for some good *consequence* of white rhinos lasting a longer rather than shorter time, we might not find one. But if we think that white rhinos are *themselves* valuable, then a world that contains them and their value for a longer time is (other things equal) better than a world with them for a shorter stretch. The fact that the lineages of alligators and horseshoe crabs go so far back in time gives them a kind of importance that more recent species lack. This does not mean that all things considered they matter more than newer species; it just means that they score higher on at least *one* dimension of value than do shorter-lived species, like the value in an ancient vase that is lacking in a newer, if more beautiful, vase.

Lenman points out that if we don't care that there are more white rhinos at *one* moment, then it is unclear why we should want more white rhinos *across* moments. Parsing this observation also requires nuance. We might question the need for adding any one individual white rhino to the population. But if we think about a *species* as a thing with its own value (a contestable but not implausible assumption), then it does matter whether we add more. Keeping all else equal, a larger rather than a medium-sized species has a size that makes it more important, just like an older species has its own special value. We should care about both the size and the duration of the species, if we care about the species at all. (Separately, as a species gets very small or very new, it can start to become distinctively important again, because it can impact other values, like the value of biodiversity.)

Size and duration may not exceed other positive qualities. Maybe they are even the least weighty of all value-conferring qualities. To Bramble's point, perhaps if expanding the overall population of white rhinos would hurt even one individual white rhino, then it's not worth it. But still, a larger individual population is apparently

18. Lenman (2002, 255–256).

more significant than a smaller one, if nobody gets hurt and all the other things are totally equal, too.

We can extend these considerations about size, duration, and beauty to power. People jockey for political power and nations seek geopolitical influence in part because they want to be significant. Bosses, teachers, judges, physicians all matter a bit more than others in their domains because they have more power. Having an outsize ability to affect other things generates its own kind of significance.

Here the welfarists will reassert their core claim. They will insist that mountains, weather, black holes, and all the other powers in the universe derive *all* their significance from impacting something of value, namely us and other sentient creatures. On this account, we are significant insofar as we and perhaps other sentient creatures have intrinsic value, and everything else gains the significance that it has entirely from its relation to valuable creatures like us: Mount Everest or a scientific discovery matters *only* because it can cause or contribute to or eliminate or help or please or harm or otherwise affect us and maybe some other creatures.

In my view, impacting welfare-enabled creatures is *one* way, but not the *only* way, that a mountain or a discovery can have value. We also judge a beautiful waterfall or a powerful celestial body valuable, even when it has not impacted us or other sentient creatures. Black holes were significant before we knew about them, and any force that smashes planets would be a significant force, even if no people, gods, Alpha Centaurians, octopi, or other welfare-enabled creatures were affected in any way. Platonism, again: we would watch a planet-smasher do its thing because it has significance; it is not significant simply because we one day wanted to watch it.

To repeat what we noted above, obviously our size and duration and power do not affect whether we matter to our mothers or communities, and these qualities do not matter *morally*. People who enjoy long lives, or who are bigger, or who are more powerful, do not deserve extra moral consideration. But this does not mean that size, power, and duration don't matter at *all*. What it instead shows is that questions of significance are not just about moral value,[19] and the inherent moral status that entitles us to being treated with respect is not the same kind of value as the intrinsic final value that we want to fill the universe with.[20] When the long lens of history proves Marie Curie to be more significant than my high school chemistry teacher, that does not mean that Curie enjoyed a higher place on some moral hierarchy. It just means she was more significant. In that respect, we should not be surprised that morally irrelevant, quantitative qualities like size, duration, and power can determine significance. Because significance can be found in *all* domains of value, not just the moral domain, we might be the most morally important creatures around but still not the most important creatures *overall*.

In fact, even welfarists like Kahane agree that the purely numerical category of *quantity* can impact significance: above we followed his lead when we established that how many instances of a thing there are—how *rare* they are—can affect their significance. On this view, if we are the only intrinsically valuable creatures in the universe, then as a *collective* we are very significant; but as one among billions each of us as an *individual* is not so significant. But if rarity can impact our significance, then why can't other quantitative properties like magnitude or duration, too? The answer seems clear—they *can*. Insofar as such final values are partly determined by rarity, they can also be shaped by other relational and quantitative properties, including size or duration or power.[21]

That said, we still must ask: How *much* value can we find at nonwelfarist sites, like the beauty of the Pillars of Creation or the power of a distant black hole or the age of the oldest dust in the cosmos? Here again, it may seem intuitive that we humans are at least the *most* important thing around: Kahane thinks that any value other

19. Metz (2013, 4).

20. Bradley (2006).

21. Relational final value (including the value of a comparative like rarity) is as final and valuable as non-relational final value (Glasgow 2023).

than the moral value contained by humans is at best "lexically inferior" to humanity's moral value.[22]

This ranking, though, goes undefended, and it may not cohere with our considered intuitions. For example, we often choose beauty over human life—for example, letting human life get extinguished by preventable causes while expending tremendous resources to preserve art—without feeling like we have imbalanced priorities. Crucially, though, for those who find such priorities ghastly, there is another approach to the question of relative value. We do not need to think that if a sufficient amount of beauty (or power or duration or size) is more *valuable* than a creature who is endowed with moral status, then that automatically means that we ought to take the step of *preserving* the beauty before we preserve a single human being. Instead we can be deontologists who think that humans have rights that demand lexical priority even over greater impersonal and overall value, in either our moral calculations or our overall rational calculations. So even bracketing how we have sacrificed morally significant creatures for morally neutral art, it is hard to see any rationale for asserting that we have greater value than everything else out there. We might have less value but still require more protection. Even if the *Mona Lisa* is more impersonally valuable than some stranger, you still have a moral obligation to save the stranger's life before rescuing the *Mona Lisa* from destruction.

* * *

Now suppose for a moment that these views about size and power and duration are incorrect. Assume instead that the *only* things that impact value are sentience, or rationality, or consciousness, or the ability to love. Or something like that—the particular details do not matter for our purposes. Would that sort of assumption make us, and perhaps other similarly endowed creatures, especially

---

22. Kahane (2014, 758).

important, if we are the only ones with those intrinsically valuable capacities in the entire cosmos? Wouldn't we then be the only value from which all other value derives? The universe would be a value-less place without us, keeping all else constant, on this assumption.

That much seems true and relevant, and it would secure one respect in which we are important. This should not be overlooked. But it is also incomplete. For there is a larger sense in which we come up short on *any* qualities that you might think make us significant—even rationality or sentience or lovingness. Our insignificance ultimately boils down to the fact that creatures like us are greatly lacking in just about *everything*. It is not just that we lack the size, duration, and difference-making power of the gods or the heroes of film and fable. It's also that our vaunted thinking and loving and agency are actually in pretty short supply, too. After all, we cannot think very well or very far. Wiping out global hunger is taking some serious time. We can't snap our fingers and create world peace. Justice is elusive.

In other words, just like we could have been much bigger or more powerful or longer-lasting, we also could have been greater sympathizers and keener knowers. Our capacity to feel and perceive is warped by cognitive distortion and limited to very narrow horizons. Even the Dalai Lama can add only a little bit of loving compassion to the universe. Making matters worse, the love we do generate is deformed by jealousy and narcissism; it is distorted by our competing passions, by our apathy and anger, by our needs and attachments.

Any argument that we have cosmic significance has to show that we have a lot of *whatever* makes things significant. We can now see how we are fated to come up short, regardless of what you prioritize in your theory of significance: for any significance-maker, we could have had so much more of it. Not only are we small, our existences brief, and our powers feeble; also we are narrow-minded and weak-willed and unloving, too, even when we are at our best, compared to how smart and kind we could have been.

THE SAGE'S ARGUMENT   *41*

You might think that this argument smuggles in an unfair standard. Why compare us to what we *could have been*?[23] Why not simply compare ourselves to the rest of the universe, as we actually are and as it actually is? In a universe that is almost entirely dark and dead and empty, we lovers and thinkers and feelers look pretty good, flawed though we may be.

To repeat the agreement that should not be overlooked: there is a truth in that thought. When we want to focus on how we matter, we rightly focus on the fact that we may be the only source of love and thought and perception in this whole place. The most important stuff that exists might be right here inside us, and if we are the *only* things with the right stuff, then that makes us cosmically important in a way. But this valorization of humanity is compatible with another angle of evaluation showing that we lack significance in another respect. This angle asks not what else is out there but instead how we could have been better than we actually are.

Both angles are relevant. Compare *justice*. Things in your part of the world may be praised as just if they are more just than the rest of the world. But they may at the same time also be condemned as unjust if they do not meet the ideal standard of how just your community's social arrangements *could* be. In the same way, we can be relatively insignificant in a universe like ours, even if we are the most significant things out there. The crumb stands out if it is the only food available, but that is small comfort if you are starving to death.

---

23. Kahane (2022). Note how evaluating our importance by comparing us counterfactually to a more valuable version of ourselves is different than the move, rejected in Chapter 2, of evaluating our importance by counterfactually replacing one person with another person in the same role. The previous evaluation from Chapter 2 kept the importance-generating *contribution* (e.g., creating calculus) stable and merely asks if counterfactually replacing or duplicating the agent responsible for that contribution (Leibniz and Newton) diminishes their significance. Now, in this chapter, we keep *you* stable and ask if counterfactually contributing more than you do contribute would have increased your importance.

In short, we make *both* actual and counterfactual comparisons when evaluating significance. We can perhaps see this better if we leave ourselves and our self-interested biases out of it and consider a universe that lacks all humans but still has arguably less valuable creatures, say dogs. In a universe where the only conscious or sentient creatures are dogs, dogs have some genuine importance. But there is a plain sense in which they are not maximally significant, because they do not add nearly as much value to the universe as could have been added if they were more valuable creatures, like us, arguably.

We regularly make such counterfactual assessments of humans, too, of course—evaluating ourselves in comparison to possible worlds where we are more valuable than we in fact are in the actual world. Viewers of *On the Waterfront* easily sympathize when Terry Malloy wails, "I coulda been a contender!" What is noteworthy is what grounds judgments like this. Malloy's importance is diminished not just by the presence of other talented fighters in the world but also by the fact that he could have been so much better than he ended up being (there is a possible world—a not unlikely possible world—where he becomes the champ). The significance of his actual accomplishments was swamped by the possibilities that had once been within reach for him. So much so that we feel bad for him—and for athletes everywhere whose injuries prevent them from ever actualizing their potential.

In the same way, our cosmic significance can be measured in two different ways. It can be compromised not just by sentient aliens from far-flung galaxies who might make our presence less crucial to the total actual value in the universe but also by the fact that we could have been more significant versions of ourselves.[24] We could have been much, much bigger. We could have been immortal. We could have had immense powers. And we could have thought more rational thoughts, loved a greater love, and sensed more sensitively, too. When we look up at the stars and feel the immense universe

---

24. For similar positions, see Benatar (2017, 49–50) and Mulgan (2015, 200).

cast our small selves as motes of dust, we imagine in these moments not *what else is hidden out there*—though we sometimes think that, too—but instead *how we could have had much more size, duration, and power than we in actuality have.* This possibility provides the footing for the common judgment that we lack cosmic significance, regardless of what one thinks the significance-makers are.

This distinction also exposes the limits of saying, "But what if the universe was smaller? Then you'd be relatively larger, and therefore more significant. So you should want the universe to shrink as much as you might want yourself to grow, or be more powerful, or longer-lasting." Any evaluation of our place in the cosmos presupposes a fixed context. When we recognize that we are cosmically small or weak, we already assume one of the parameters of evaluation, namely the scale of the actual cosmos. We are not imagining how different the universe could have been, keeping ourselves fixed—how important we would be on a *different scale.* Instead we are establishing the universe's scale roughly as it is and then imagining how different *we* could have been on that scale.

Again, sometimes we do the other thing, too, where we imagine the world, rather than ourselves, differently. *Maybe I would have gotten that job, if my rival hadn't applied, too. I could have set a new record if it hadn't been so windy that day.* When we do this, rather than highlighting our own insignificance, we instead highlight the significance of the universe around us. Doing this is compatible with the fact that we *also* ask why we aren't as powerful or big or long-lasting or smart or loving as we could have been.[25]

* * *

25. A similar response is available to the argument that making significance dependent on long duration is an unreasonable standard because surely we can get significance just from short-term results (Trisel 2004). It is true that we can get *some* significance from short-term impact. But that does not mean that modest significance is enough for cosmic significance. Cosmic significance does require huge impacts, and very long—perhaps eternal—duration. That requirement is baked right into evaluations made about a cosmos like ours.

So is there any hope that we might find something about us that could make us cosmically significant, even though we are not only small and weak and short-lived but also limited lovers and thinkers and feelers? One enticing possibility for boosting our significance to cosmic levels is to insist that there is some significance-maker that we *necessarily* have a lot of. For instance, if being human were by itself enough to make us cosmically significant, then we are flush with significance. There is no way that we could be more human than we are, and nothing in the universe could be more human than we are. The problem with this suggestion, though, is that being human per se is an unpromising candidate for a significance-generator. Being a human as opposed to, say, a cow or a shoe or some helium, is just a detail of taxonomy. And it is hard to see why any given taxonomic detail might be a significance-maker.

Now instead we could construe what is distinctive about humanity in a non-taxonomic, evaluatively charged way, as important traditions say when they tell us that humanity in the sense of having rational capacity, or perhaps sentience, is a basis for having moral status. But then we are back to our earlier point. These traditions capture ways in which we matter, and matter more than a shoe. But even if that is correct, it equally remains true that we could have had much greater significance on the rationality and sentience fronts. Just as we could have been larger, we could have felt much more pleasure or been much more sensitive to smell and sound or had much greater powers of understanding. And we could have had the power to bestow rationality or sentience upon shoes. Now *that* would be significant.

The last potential source of significance to consider comes from those religious views where we have some god-given purpose. Although this book pursues the question of human insignificance from a secular perspective, it is easy to see how this religious approach might seem especially tempting as a way to vindicate the Significance Impulse, since the search for meaning just is, for many, the search for some sort of justifiable purpose to our existence.[26] It promises a double win: it tells us how we can be important—get a purpose from a god!—and why it is in our interests—it is The Meaning of Life!

If, like Ali and Williams, you want to be especially important as an individual, then on this approach some god would have to give you your own special, individual purpose, something that is of higher value than what the rest of us have. If, instead, you are content for humanity at large to be important while you individually remain relatively inessential, then we would need some collective purpose of high value. For the kind of secular philosophy being pursued in this book, the prospects are dim for such purposes. From that perspective it is hard to find a good reason to believe that any one person has such a purpose, let alone a purpose that is more important than others have. Similarly, it is hard to find a good reason to think that we have any collective purpose. At best this proposal makes our situation sound similar to Frankl's ape, which suffers because we are experimenting on it for scientific gain: its suffering has a real and valuable purpose, but it cannot know what that purpose is.[27] This always struck me as a bad deal for the ape.

In addition, significance that comes from being another agent's purposive instrument is not the kind of significance that satisfies the Significance Impulse. Us being a cog in another's machine, a player in someone else's drama, a tool in some other agent's workshop makes *them* important. We, by contrast, are relegated to being mere instruments for that external force, while that force is what has the real value.[28]

---

26. For example, Benatar (2017, 50).

27. Frankl (1959, 119–120).

28. Nagel (1971, 721); Dworkin (2013, 216); Baier (1957, 20). See also Brogaard and Smith (2005); Fischer (2020, 6); Kahane (2011, 683); Kekes (1986); Kitcher (2014, 106–108); Nozick (1981, 586); Taylor (1987).

THE SIGNIFICANCE IMPULSE

Though some emphasize that a certain kind of god might still very much *care* for us,[29] the loss of autonomy is a concern regardless. Even if the purpose imposed on me was *my own happiness*,[30] I am not particularly keen on someone or something else deciding for me that this is my purpose, rather than any of the other purposes I might choose for myself. And for the record, I love being happy—it is one of my favorite states of being! But maybe I would choose to advance justice at the cost of my own happiness, or to sacrifice my own happiness for my child's, or to become wiser even though it painfully awakens me to the misery in the world. We need to adopt our own purpose in order for that purpose to add value to our lives. We must chart our own paths.

Of course, there are good reasons to fear that we may not be wholly autonomous. Our choices spring not just from coolly and rationally assessing our options but also from nature, nurture, and the tech bros' algorithms. Still, choosing our purposes, even if our choices are themselves externally molded, seems vastly preferable to having purposes chosen for us. Shallow autonomy might not be as good as deep autonomy, but it's better than no autonomy at all. In fact, even if a god made *being autonomous* our purpose, that attempt to have it both ways would not solve our problem. A purpose can be externally given, or it can be self-given; but it can't be both at the same time.[31]

So we do not have the kind of evidence we need to believe that we have some externally given purpose. And even if we did, it would strip us of our autonomy, making this purpose alien to our selves

---

29. Luper (2014, 202).

30. Goetz and Seachris (2016, 3).

31. For more on these issues, see Mawson (2016). Sartre (1946) maintained that self-creation is what gives us a dignity that exceeds the value of a mere tool. He hangs our "greater dignity" on the promise of deep autonomy, where we can be full self-creators; but again, even the value of shallow autonomy gives us reason to reject an externally imposed purpose as inauthentic.

and thereby diminishing its value for us. And even if it somehow didn't do that, it would still undermine our importance by making us wholly subordinate to the external purpose-imposer.

* * *

At least collectively—though not individually—we do have a real kind of significance if we are the only consciousnesses in existence. We do have value. But even though that is true, still we barely register on the scales of cosmic significance. Our importance drowns in a sea of capacity. We remain the puny kid in the back of an empty room, if the room was about the size of the universe. The sage's argument for our cosmic insignificance remains intact.

4

Living Your Best Life

So far we have seen how we are relatively unimportant on the grandest scale. As observed earlier, many find this thought terrifying, concluding that our lives are doomed. We turn now to an antidote to that negativity. The arguments that follow open up a different, more optimistic outlook, first with the claim that being cosmically important would not have made things better for us anyway and then with the argument that being unimportant actually allows us to gain certain goods, too.

As we explore how importance might benefit us, it helps to adopt language that marks the different kinds of interests we have. Consider Nelson Mandela. As Mandela languished for years on Robben Island, he wasn't doing particularly well. In addition to the brutal prison conditions, he spent nearly three decades separated from everything he loved. The experience was a tremendous sacrifice of well-being. But arguably, it added *meaning* to his life to give up so much well-being in order to advance the cause of justice in apartheid South Africa.[1] I will label considerations of mean-

---

1. See, for example, Benatar (2017, 65). For a recent analysis of the gap between prudential well-being and meaning in life, see Hammerton (2022).

The Significance Impulse. Joshua Glasgow, Oxford University Press. © Oxford University Press 2024.
DOI: 10.1093/9780197754788.003.0004

ing, well-being, and any other benefits to ourselves our "personal interests." This label is meant to contrast our own interests with the impersonal interest we have in, say, making the world a better place—which is good to do but may not always be in one's own personal interests. But just in terms of his own personal interests, Mandela's sacrifice can seem to advance the *meaning* he drew from life while nonetheless diminishing his distinct interest in having high levels of *well-being*.

Now it is tempting to think that the importance of what Mandela did is exactly what gave so much meaning to his sacrifice. We will return to the relationship between importance and meaning in Chapter 5. In this chapter we first ask whether being important improves the *well-being* of the important person. The combined conclusion of these two chapters will be that being important by itself advances neither the meaning in your life nor your well-being, nor (to generalize from there) any other personal interest of yours. And this means that it is not bad for us to be the crumbs of cosmic value that we are.

Before diving into the claim that being important by itself advances none of our personal interests, it is worth re-emphasizing that we do have some reasons besides serving our own self-interest to try to be important. That is to say, even if we have no *personal* reason to do something significant, still we do have those *impersonal* reasons for doing so. Mandela might well have chosen to sacrifice his personal well-being not because doing so made *his* life more meaningful but just because it was a good thing to do for *others*. He might have been motivated by a judgment that his sacrifice was his moral duty, and any gain in making his life more meaningful would just be a side effect of trying to do the right thing. And there are, of course, other impersonal reasons to act. For example, our tortured artist might create their art just because they believe that they have impersonal aesthetic reasons to add beauty to the world, even if doing so makes them personally miserable.

So there seem to be impersonal, non-self-interested reasons we have to try to do important things. And on the self-interest front, it is also worth recalling that being important often comes attached to certain social rewards that we do have *personal* reason to secure. Sometimes people seem to benefit from the money, fame, influence, and adoration that come their way for doing something truly remarkable. Other things equal, it seems worth pursuing these goods. Of course, in the final accounting other things are never equal. Any comprehensive evaluation of being important must also factor in the costs of importance—the risks to privacy, mental and physical health, family integrity, and more—as well as the ways that money, fame, and influence can deform our priorities when handled poorly. But those counterbalances notwithstanding, the prizes we attach to significance can still be, well, significant.

And society is arguably savvy to award those prizes.[2] Living in a place where people do important things is better for us than living in a place where people only do ordinary things. We collectively benefit when individuals create groundbreaking music or liberate their people from oppression or forestall the destruction of our planet. Especially since such efforts can cost people the benefits of a more well-rounded life, compensating their significant action greases the gears of progress. Soothing the corrosive consequences of being important with rewards incentivizes people to make our world better in grander ways. But again, these benefits (and costs) that society attaches to being important do not tell us anything about the benefits of being important per se. The issue we are tackling is whether importance *itself* is in our interests. To examine that question, we must factor out those social rewards. So let's start with a hypothetical case that does just that, to give life to the Significance Impulse.

---

2. That said, how these rewards ought to be doled out is a difficult question of social policy (Woodruff 2014).

Imagine that as a twenty-year-old starts to plan out her fore-seeable adulthood, she must choose between a relatively routine trajectory—say, motherhood and a career as an effective if com-pletely normal elementary school teacher—and a more impactful path—a career in educational politics that could get her elected to a very high office. She thinks she should pursue the political career because she has a realistic shot at transforming the entire educa-tion system for the better. This is a delicate calculation on her part. She doesn't want fame; in fact, she prefers privacy. Her loved ones provide her with all the adoration she needs, and she shyly recoils at getting too much attention. She recently won the lottery and has concluded that she now has way more money than she could ever realistically want. She avoids power because experience has shown her that it tempts her to make choices that compromise her integrity. In sum, for this woman, the socially attached prizes of following the significant path are unenticing and irrelevant. But despite the fact that none of the contingently attached social incentives inspire her to be important, she chooses to take the more important path any-way. In making this choice, she also is not motivated by a sense of moral duty; she is not pursuing the important path for impersonal reasons. Instead, she is drawn to the idea that it would be in her own personal interests to be a somebody rather than a nobody. Being important is something she values for herself, even if the costs of doing so are substantial. The way she sees things, an important life is a better life to live than an ordinary life. The Significance Impulse courses through her.

Is she right? When the socially attached rewards of importance are removed from consideration, is it still in our interests to be important? Obviously, there's no point struggling for something that is totally worthless; we should only bother striving for valuable pursuits. But why must those *valuable* efforts be *especially signifi-cant*? If a social worker fights to get a home for an unhoused student, or if an inventor struggles to create a gentler dental instrument—or if our twenty-year-old takes the routine path and teaches children well—why is their project not as choice-worthy, from the perspective of self-interest, as the Nobel Prize winner's grander achievement? To repeat, here we look for a kind of choice-worthiness that is choice-worthy not for humanity, nor for moral reasons, nor for the greater good, but just for *the interests of the person involved in the pursuit*. What *personal* reason does the twenty-year-old have to pursue importance, once she disavows the prizes?

In order to firm up our grip on where we might find the personal interest in being important, return now to our earlier case: How would you feel if you turn out to be the person who eliminates cancer? Suppose that a trickster offers a pair of outcomes, one each to you and your next-door neighbor. One of you will be an extraordinary person, creating a cheap pill that cures cancer. (And along with it there is a solution to the problem of diminishing resources that will result from the expanding population.) This person will have one of history's rarest, most valuable impacts, in the running for the Greatest of All Time. The other will be an ordinary person—a neighborhood pharmacy clerk who dispenses medicine, including some of those cancer-curing pills. As before, whoever cures cancer, part of the deal is that no public recognition is attached to this towering achievement because the jerk who runs the cancer research lab will falsely claim all the credit, and everyone will believe him.[3] So neither you nor your neighbor will get recognition or riches for curing cancer; then again, the upside is that neither of you will experience the hassles of fame, either. In this version of the story, each career will last the same amount of time and require the same demands of your personal life; and let us assume that you like both careers equally—you find scientific research stimulating, but you also are a "people person" who would enjoy directly interfacing with and helping customers at the pharmacy. Finally, both careers pay

---

3. In case this sounds like a ridiculous impossibility, recall the episode when Jocelyn Bell Burnell discovered pulsars but the Nobel Prize went to her supervisor and *his* supervisor but not to her (Proudfoot 2021). Or when Crick and Watson claimed Rosalind Franklin's share of the DNA limelight.

the same, except for one wrinkle added by the trickster: at retirement the pharmacy clerk will get a $1 bonus. From the perspective of self-interest, $1 is the only discernably different consequence between the two paths, besides the fact that one is ordinary and the other extraordinary. One measly dollar is the only contingently attached external reward (or penalty) in play, and it goes to the pharmacist rather than the curer of cancer.

In this scenario considerations of better or worse outcomes for the world are off the table because, either way, someone is curing cancer. So assuming that no other *impersonal* reasons are relevant, the only consideration left to weigh is your *personal* self-interest. Is it in your own interests to be the (under-the-radar) hero who cures cancer? Or is it better to live an ordinary life and get that $1 bonus? The trickster tosses a coin, and you get to be the curer of cancer. How should you feel?

The Significance Impulse, of course, tells us that we should be thrilled to be the one who cures cancer; it makes it seem almost stupid to chase $1 while leaving G.O.A.T. status on the table. But that verdict would be a mistake, according to the argument in the rest of this chapter. The two paths are actually equally in our self-interest, except for that $1 bonus. And so because of the $1 bonus, you should prefer to be the pharmacy clerk instead of the person who cures cancer. That dollar makes it better to be the sidekick than the hero. Being the G.O.A.T. is not itself a life worth aiming for. The Significance Impulse has us chasing fool's gold.

We have limited options when trying to defend or disprove such a claim. It is particularly hard to establish that something does *not* exist, which is what I am saying when I say that you have no self-interested reason to be important. We can appeal to your sense of modesty: Why should *you* be such a big deal? But that can only carry us so far in our ego-driven world. Then there is the gap between the impersonal value of important things happening and the personal value that you might reap if you end up as the important person: we definitely should want a world where important things happen, and we may have some impersonal responsibility to help make those important things happen; but that does not mean that it is in your personal interests for you to be that important person, as opposed to someone else occupying the important role. But those in the grip of the Significance Impulse will insist that some interest of ours *is* in fact served by being important. So what we must do is lay out our interests and examine how being important might advance them. If we cannot find any such advantage, then we can tentatively conclude that none of our interests are served by being important.

*   *   *

There are two views that we must sideline. They can easily explain why it might benefit us to be important. But they do not get to the heart of our question.

The first sidelined answer can be found in a now-famous speech by the mathematician and scientist Richard Hamming. He was encouraging other scientists to do first-class work—the truly exceptional stuff that wins Nobel Prizes—on the grounds that doing something significant is, he claimed, "worthwhile in itself." That is to say, nothing *makes* being important good for us, on this account. It *just is* good for us. It is a *final* good: something we should want for ourselves not because it secures some further good but just because of what it is in itself.

Now obviously some things do appear to be final goods. Gaining knowledge or feeling pleasure seems good for us, not necessarily because these things lead to or contribute to any other good but just because they are among the things that are ultimately good for us. Being important is like this, according to Hamming: there is nothing that *makes* being important worthwhile; it just *is* worthwhile. And if being important, like getting pleasure, has final value for us, then being the one to cure cancer would be good for you just because it makes you important, in the way that eating ice cream is good for us just because it is pleasurable: we don't need any further rationale for pursuing it once it promises to deliver the final good in question.

The trick in classifying any particular good as a *final* good is to convince us that this classification is correct without undermining the finality of the value. With most of our pursuits we can spell out some *reason* why they are worth our time and effort. Why go to work? Because you need an income. Why secure an income? Because you need shelter for your family. And so on. At some point this chain of values must end at a final good: you seek shelter for your family because shelter is required for happiness, and happiness is the last good in the chain, end of story. Because this is the end of the story, we cannot use our usual tool of giving a further value-based rationale for valuing the final good, in this case the good of happiness. Pleasure is good, period; knowledge is good, period; beauty is good, period. There is no further reason to pursue those goods—that's what makes them *final* goods.

For our inquiry into the merits of the Significance Impulse, we can (and should) accept that there are final goods; but we cannot adopt Hamming's more specific claim that being important is one of those final goods. For one thing, it is not obvious that being important is like pleasure or knowledge, in this respect. When we run into people like Kahlo, who do not value being important, we are interested in seeing if we can find some *reason* for them to be important. By contrast, we don't feel so tempted to supply that sort of reason to someone who doesn't want pleasure. With someone who insists that pleasure is not good, we can only accept that we are at an impasse and regret that they do not appreciate one of life's final goods. With Kahlo and Williams, by contrast, we are tempted to look for an argument that one side is right. Providing such a rationale (typically, at least) amounts to pointing to a further value and therefore giving up the alleged finality of the good.

And more fundamentally, since we are taking seriously the possibility that there is no reason of self-interest to be important, insisting without any rationale that importance has its own final value cannot really be an effective answer to our particular question. The moment we decided to look for a reason why we should care about being important, we already shelved the possibility that it has final value. So making the assumption that importance has final value will not help us find what we are looking for—and worse, that move would fallaciously assume what needs to be proven, in this context. That said, we can flip this point in a more ecumenical direction that might appeal to someone like Hamming: if we conclude that none of our other personal interests are advanced by being important, then the only way that being important might benefit us is if it is a final good. That is, the value in being important would have to be inexplicable and outside the bounds of rational evaluation. That we can agree on.

The other theory that we must sideline *does* offer a reason to value being important. This reason lies entirely within us: we have reason to be important simply because we *want* to be important. J. David Velleman wrote in one of his books, "I would be thrilled to learn that this essay would still be read a million years hence."[4] Given that this outcome would thrill Velleman, isn't it good for him if it comes true and people are still reading his book in a million years? On one theory of what is good for us, it is good to get what we want. Plausibly, then, if people want to be important, it is good for them to be important. So if Ali and Williams want to be important, then being important benefits them; and if Kahlo doesn't want to be important, then being important does not benefit her.

Let's concede the subjectivist principle that if you want something, then other things equal it is good for you to get it. I question whether this is true, since it seems like we want to want what is desirable for some good reason, as opposed to what we want being desirable simply because we want it.[5] But I am happy to grant for the sake of argument the basic subjectivist idea that it benefits people to

4. Velleman (2015, 120).

5. Scanlon (2000).

get what they want. Even with that concession, again our project is to figure out what we *should* want for ourselves. Yes, our lives may be better to the degree that we get what we want, other things being equal. But that does not tell me if my wants are well placed—if other things are in fact equal.

As before, we could be robust objectivists about the standards that govern our wants and conclude that our preferences must fit a completely mind-independent regime of values. But another way to think about the goal of having well-placed wants, one that is more comfortable for some subjectivists, is that *merely* wanting something does not make getting it good for me *all things considered*. It is probably not in the addict's interests *overall* to get their hands on a drug that makes people euphoric for a moment before killing them. It is probably not in the overall interests of a confused thirsty person to satisfy a desire to guzzle bleach. And it's probably not in your interests, overall, to get to be with the one you love, if they are just trying to get their hands on your fortune when you die. Being happy, getting pleasure, and fulfilling our desires, preferences, and goals may have some goodness for us; but for plausible forms of subjectivism, getting what you want is ultimately in your interests only when balanced against your *other* wants.[6]

One of those other wants, a fairly dominant other interest, is in having our desires *make sense*. If I want to watch paint dry, I also (subjectively) think that I ought to consider whether watching paint dry is a valuable use of my time. A robust anti-subjectivist might insist that watching paint dry is *really, objectively* a waste of time. But a more subjectivist-friendly variation on the same theme simply notes that watching paint dry is not how I would *reflectively, coherently, and with full information* choose to spend my time. There are plenty of interesting and difficult questions to ask about which is the best evaluation of acting on the desire to watch paint dry. We can sidestep those. What is crucial for us is that for satisfying a

---

6. Heathwood (2005); Keller (2004).

desire to be in our overall interests, it has to answer to some sort of standard that says that the object of our desire is *worth* wanting—a standard that exists outside of that isolated desire.

In this spirit, our project is to see if the Significance Impulse is *worth* our endorsement. For us, it is not enough for being important to be something we want. It is not enough just to feel the pull of the Significance Impulse. We already know that many people want to be important. What we seek here is confidence that this desire is somehow justifiable. For us to actually expend our resources and take on real risks to become significant, even if we are just risking the trickster's $1 bonus, it has to be worth wanting. We want to know that we are *right* to want to be important—that, at a minimum, being important gets us something we want for ourselves.

So because we are trying to find out if we have any good reason to want to be important, our task cannot be completed by insisting that importance either is a final good or is merely something we want. Instead, the challenge of vindicating the Significance Impulse is to show that some of our interests might be served by being important—making it so that we have some good personal reason to want to be important.

The first candidate personal reason to be important, explored next, is that it uniquely enables us to live our best lives.

* * *

Finding the cure for a disease, creating a new form of music, advancing civil rights: these are ways of being important, and they are also achievements. So we might think of importance as the flip side of achievement in the sense that any big achievement is going generate rare and high value for the achiever. And many have argued that living a life with achievements is better for us than living a life of continuous cartoon-watching. Putting these thoughts together, if achievements add value to our lives, and if being important goes hand in hand with achievement, then it looks like we do have a reason of self-interest to be significant.

There is an ambiguity in "achievement." We sometimes use that word to refer to *great* achievement. Usain Bolt's running records stand as a towering achievement in this sense. Dolores Huerta organizing farmworkers was a tremendous achievement, too. But there is also a separate sense of achievement. Becoming a master carpenter, cataloguing all the species of ringworm in North America, raising well-functioning children, moving to another country with nothing so that your family can secure a better life: these are all achievements, too. Call these relatively pedestrian—if remarkable—achievements "standard" achievements.

Because some achievements are merely standard while others are great, any link between achievement and personal value is not by itself strong enough to vindicate the Significance Impulse. If you build yourself a mountain cabin using only hand-powered tools and the resources on the land, that achievement arguably adds value to your life. So does becoming a medical doctor. So does creating a successful after-school program for at-risk kids. But achieving these things would not make you especially important, someone of extraordinarily high and rare value, someone like Gandhi or Cervantes.[7] More precisely, standard achievement actually can make us important when the scope of evaluation is contextually restricted: you are important to the kids at that school or the patients in your medical practice. But standard achievements do not make us very important in the grander schemes. They do not make us important on the national or global or historic or universal stage. The value in standard achievements just isn't that kind of value. It might be terribly valuable for us personally to achieve something, but that does not make the personally valuable achievement cosmically important. In short, *achievement itself* doesn't guarantee

---

7. As is consistently recognized by those who work on achievement (Bradford 2015, 2; 2016, 797; Portmore 2007, 5–6; Griffin 1986, 65).

60   THE SIGNIFICANCE IMPULSE

importance, so to whatever extent achieving things makes our lives go well for us, it will not ensure that importance also makes our lives go well for us.

Now some add that, other things equal, we should want for our lives to contain the *greatest* achievements possible.[8] So next let us narrow our focus to specifically great achievement. What sets great achievements apart from standard achievements is that they have one of the significance-makers. For Huerta, the significance-maker is improving the health, social power, and material living conditions of so many workers and their families, giving her life an importance that outshines the PTA dad who organizes a push to get rid of sugary drinks in his kid's school. Her life is the more impactful and important one.

But what special *personal* interest does Huerta secure that the PTA dad lacks? It is not in the mere fact of achievement itself, for that is common to both Huerta and the PTA parent. Of course, Huerta may take more *felt satisfaction* from her efforts than the PTA parent does (although, also, she may not), but that is merely a subjective reward of the kind that we set aside earlier. And although Huerta's work has more *moral* value, that does not explain why her achievement advances *her own* interests more than the PTA parent's advances his own interests. Though these are famously vexed issues, I am in the camp that believes that people who are immoral can nonetheless often serve their own self-interests and that being moral can often come at the cost of tremendous personal sacrifice. Rather than wading deep into that question, it is enough for us here to observe that if a defense of the Significance Impulse relies on, first, the premise that being moral always contributes to one's self-interest and, second, the further premise that being *more* moral always adds *more* to one's self-interest than does being less moral, then proving the prudential value of importance is going to be an uphill slog.

So return to the apparent personally rewarding aspects of achievement. We might get more personal value from an achieve-

8. Hurka (2011, 60).

ment by *investing* more in it or *working* harder or *overcoming* more difficulty or *exercising our capacities* to a greater degree.[9] All that can be true and, still, the achievement's level of *importance* does not seem to add any extra benefit beyond the benefit we reap from those other elements in the achievement. That is, we might pack a great achievement full of hard work or overcoming difficulty, but those qualities might just as well be present in a standard achievement. Consequently, while we arguably have an interest in setting a difficult goal and then realizing it, it is unclear that beyond the achievement value, it is also true that the more valuable that goal, the more well-being we personally accumulate.[10] Not for nothing, this would explain why Huerta, like many other important figures, says that her greatest achievement was the very ordinary accomplishment of raising her kids, rather than improving millions of strangers' lives.[11] Presumably she is saying that in terms of the value she has reaped for *herself*, for her own life, the ordinary achievement of parenting was more valuable than her extraordinary achievement of advancing justice and well-being across a society.

So there appears to be no reason to think that the greater our achievement, the more we increase our own personal well-being. Achievement is (arguably) in our interests, but it is not necessarily important in our sense, while specifically *great* achievement is important in our sense but appears to serve no extra self-interest beyond the personal interests that are already served by standard achievements. Achieving truly great things does not by itself make your life any better than achieving standard things does.

---

9. Dunkle (2019); Hirji (2019); Keller (2004, 34); Portmore (2007). What, exactly, makes achievement valuable? Do we care about effort per se, or is difficulty or the amount of investment or sacrifice we put in what really makes something a valuable achievement? Is it about exercising one's will or rationality or some other capacity? See also Bradford (2015, 2016); Hurka (1993); von Kriegstein (2017).

10. Bradford (2016, 798–799).

11. Huerta (2006, 17).

Now securing achievements is not the only way of being your best self. Flourishing, for example, is more about actualizing your inner potential than it is about achieving results. One way to construe this goal is as aiming to perfect your general human nature, physically and rationally.[12] But pretty clearly this, too, does not give us reason to be important. To whatever extent there is value in becoming the best human you can be, your life may still be quite ordinary. It is conceivable and—given the rarity of important people—even likely that, in all of human history, the person who has most perfected human nature was relatively unimportant. There is no reason to think that important people have a better chance at perfecting human nature than the rest of the species has.

It is tempting to think that there are more and less rewarding ways of exercising your capacities. For instance, if you do something that is more elaborate or complex, you are probably going to develop your rationality more than if you do something simple.[13] But even if we allow that doing *complex* things is better for you—although just speaking for my sunset-watching, cards-playing, beer-drinking self, the simple things in life seem pretty great, too—this still does not mean that it is in our interest to do *important* things. After all, complex and elaborate projects are not equivalent to important projects. Curing a disease that kills millions is very important, but it is not necessarily a greater exercise of rationality than curing a rare and only slightly annoying fungal infection. Planning out a really amazing year of school for your twenty-five ten-year-old students can be just as complex as planning a protest that advances social justice for a whole nation. Being important and exercising rationality are different things, and so gains in the latter are not guaranteed to positively correlate with gains in the former.

Instead of focusing on *general* human capacities like rationality, we might understand flourishing as optimizing your *distinctive*

12. Hurka (1993).

13. Hurka (1993).

LIVING YOUR BEST LIFE

individual talents. Perhaps what we should want for ourselves is to fulfill our unique potential, to develop the distinctive capacities that separate each of us from the rest of the pack. According to this view, if Coltrane's specific capacity is to change music in a profound way, then it was in his own self-interest to fulfill that promise. And when he succeeded, he did something hugely significant. Isn't this a rationale for trying to be important?[14]

In a roundabout way, all of these positions we are canvassing do tap into something indisputable. Maximizing our potential *is* a reason to do something that might lead to importance. If we should try to realize our potential, then the people who have the potential to do important things will, if they succeed, ultimately be important. The same goes for those for whom perfecting human nature would, coincidentally, lead to important things or whose achievements would, coincidentally, generate important results: if successful, they will wind up important. And it explains why we think that folks like Coltrane have self-interested reasons to do their important deeds. In addition to the *impersonal* reasons to do important things—such as moral value or, for many important works of art and science, purely aesthetic and epistemic value—we can recognize that the artist or scientist has personal reasons to maximize their individual potential. If you have the potential to do something valuable, then it is in your interests to do that. And by that reasoning, if you can do something *really* valuable, that is, important, then it is in your interests to actualize that potential, too.

But this is equally a personal reason to do something *less* valuable, too, if that is where your personal potential finds its limit. The imperative to be all you can be is not a reason to be important per se. It is just a reason to realize your potential. While we should all be glad that Coltrane did what he did, the realize-your-unique-potential theory gives him no reason to be extra excited that his way of realizing his potential was important, beyond how

14. For discussion of these sorts of views, see Gewirth (1998); Gilabert (2022); Tiberius (2008, 3).

more ordinary people should feel about realizing their more pedestrian potentials. Realizing one's own potential is something that all of us can do; what we differ in is what our potential is.

Contrast Coltrane with Joe Dullstain. What Dullstain does best is get a pleasantly flat finish into matte paints—he does this better than anyone at the local paint shop, and he does it better than he does anything else in his life. Coltrane and Dullstain actualize their individual potential to the same degree: they fulfill it maximally. Of course, because Coltrane's capacities promise more importance than what is available with Dullstain's capacities, Coltrane winds up more important than Dullstain. But in terms of maxing out their own individual capacities, both Coltrane and Dullstain are flourishing equally. According to the live-up-to-your-individual-potential principle, the two of them are thriving *equally* insofar as they each do all that they can do. That is how the value of individual flourishing fails to entail that being important is in our interests. If you reach your highest capacity and if, like Coltrane, you thereby change the world, then you will have served your self-interests—but no more than ordinary Dullstain serves his self-interests by reaching his highest capacity. All three of you will flourish equally in the operative sense since all three of you equally maximize your unique potentials.

The fulfill-your-individual-potential principle focuses only on our ability to fulfill our capacities. It fails to evaluate or rank the capacities themselves, which is why that principle cannot show that we have a personal interest in being important as opposed to flourishing in relatively unimportant ways. So let us now consider a different view that does have such a ranking. In fact, some of the greats themselves held this alternative view. They believed that in addition to the value in fulfilling our potential, it is a benefit to have higher-ranked capacities (whatever those may be). Aristotle, for example, thought that you needed the luck of being born with high capacities to get the best possible life.[15] And Nietzsche wrote

15. Aristotle (1999, NE 1100b22–1101a8); cf. Hurka (1993, 59).

that your life gets "the highest value and deepest significance" and is minimally "squandered" if it is among "the rarest and most valuable types" of our species.[16] This variation on the self-realization argument for the value of importance is that, in addition to maximally fulfilling our individual capacities, we should want our capacities to be maximally valuable. Wouldn't you rather have a life with Coltrane's ceiling than one with Dullstain's?

Part of the problem with this particular pro-greatness argument is that if our capacities set the chief value of our lives, then once our capacities start to diminish we will have less reason to go on living.[17] That seems incorrect. Additionally, it is not clear why we should think that having high capacities itself is something that benefits us. To be sure, there are several reasons to want to have Coltrane's capacities. Creative work is rewarding in itself, as any starving artist will testify. And pushing through barriers you've never previously broken is worth it, too, as any persistent striver will report. But those are things that Dullstain can experience as much as Coltrane can. They are not reasons for having an extraordinary artistic talent with unusual breakthrough capacities. The values in creativity and hard work are reasons for having capacities with *that* character; they make room for invention and demanding effort. But that alone does not give us reason to have capacities that might yield *greatness*.

If you want maximal capacities for yourself, then you should want to have not only Coltrane's ability to create beautiful music but also Dullstain's capacities for making luxurious matte paints, too. And that would be ridiculous; it is fine if you don't care about that capacity. Personally, I see no value in my having the ability to create beautiful matte finishes; I am happy to leave that one to Dullstain. Nor do I care about being a quick draw or a powerful pole vaulter or a really keen urban planner. Let's not fetishize capacity. I personally like making music more than I like making paints or city plans, so

16. Nietzsche (1873, sec. 6).

17. Hurka (1993, chap. 6).

66   THE SIGNIFICANCE IMPULSE

I value Coltrane's capacities more than the alternatives; but plenty of other people have other preferences, and they would rather have the capacities that allow them to flourish with their endeavors. It is thus hard to see how having maximal as opposed to routine capacities is supposed to augment our personal well-being.

* * *

So it looks like there is no way to harness the value of flourishing or achievement to prove that we should want to be important. But as a last move, maybe the imperative to live our best lives has a more direct connection to being important. Maybe it is just good for us to connect to value in a certain way: even if someone else would fix climate change instead of you, you want to be the one to do so because it matters to you how *you* interact with value. We ought to try to be the link between the world and positive value, on this line of thought.

Now if this claim is not simply another version of the idea that maximally connecting one's life to positive value is just a final good—a view we sidelined at the top of this chapter—then we still have to provide some *reason* to think that such a link is valuable. One way to provide such a reason is to argue by analogy: trying to be the link between the world and positive value appears to be symmetrical with a role we want to *avoid*, namely being the link between the world and evil.[18] Imagine that a terrorist tells you that they will kill one innocent stranger unless you kill some other innocent stranger. It matters to most of us to not bloody our hands; you would refuse to comply with the terrorist's threat because either you don't want to be the one to produce extreme disvalue or you more basically just do not want to kill. We think it is bad to be the conduit for evil, even when we can be certain that the evil is going to happen one way or another. In fact, many of us find this sort of agent-relative obligation so powerful that we continue to endorse

---

18. Thanks to Douglas Portmore for pressing this line in conversation.

it as the numbers get worse: even if the terrorist threatened to kill *five* innocent strangers unless you kill one, you might still refuse on the grounds that you cannot be the kind of person who goes around killing innocent people.

The issues in play here are also well known for their difficulty. To stay on the question of our significance, we can keep our task manageable by focusing on the fact that we do feel the pull of these agent-relative demands on our actions.[19] We want to minimize our connections to evil. So, the symmetry argument continues, doesn't consistency require that we try to maximize our connections to good, too? Shouldn't we want to advance positive value as much as we want to avoid doing evil in our own lives? If so, then we would seem to have a reason to be important: being important is simply a byproduct of optimizing our personal connection to positive value. If you try to maximize your relation to what is good, and if you succeed more than most in this endeavor by producing a *ton* of what is good, then you will be of especially high and rare positive value. You will be important.

But it is not clear how to deliver the supposed parity between reasons to do good and reasons to avoid doing evil. Crucially, it seems that these reasons are actually *asymmetrical*: our reasons to avoid evil seem to have a different character than our reasons to seek the good. Other asymmetries indicate as much. For example, I'd feel much more guilty about doing something very harmful than doing something only slightly harmful, but that gap dissipates when it comes to doing good: if I do something only slightly beneficial, I shouldn't (and don't) feel nearly as guilty about not also doing something very beneficial instead. Or for another point of asymmetry, would we prefer to feed one hungry child if that prevents another agent from feeding two hungry children (keeping all else equal)? In the doing-good case, once I know that these are the only two possibilities and that the more advantageous possibility is being

19. Scheffler (1982).

secured by someone else, it seems like any reason I have to feed the hungry child is canceled. But the parallel reasoning does not hold up in the avoiding-evil case: I continue to avoid killing an innocent person even if doing so would prevent a terrorist from killing two other innocent people. This, again, is what generates the puzzle about agent-relative restrictions on wrongdoing. Tellingly, no such paradox arises for agent-relative obligations to promote the good.

Thus, while at first glance it might seem like our reason to seek positive value is symmetrical with our reason to avoid negative value, further investigation indicates that the two sorts of reasons are actually asymmetrical. And so we cannot use that analogy to show that we have reasons of self-interest to be important, even if we do have personal reasons to minimize the evil we produce (and, for that matter, even if we also have *impersonal* reasons to maximize the good). These considerations suggest that to be concerned with how *our own* lives connect to the positive value in the world, rather than being concerned with what important value is in the world regardless of who gets to be the conduit of that value, exaggerates the significance of one's own personal connection to value.

5

Meaning

One rationale for the Significance Impulse is especially popular: the more important you are—you improve the health of millions, create amazing new art, liberate your people from oppression—the more *meaningful* your life is supposed to be.

For some, this relationship between importance and meaning follows from a semantic stipulation that a meaningful life is by *definition* a life that is important, significant, or impactful or has some purpose that matters.[1] Others stop short of saying that importance is part of the very definition of meaning in life but still claim that achieving something important is *necessary* for securing meaning.[2]

---

1. Bennett (1984, 582); Martela (2017); Metz (2002, 801; 2013, 18, 21, 187, 247); Nozick (1981, 575); Smuts (2013, 547–548).

2. A. J. Ayer (1190, 196) holds that a meaningful life "is a matter of one's standing in one's society and the historical influence, if any, that one exerts," and Kurt Baier (1957, 27–29) argues that to lead a meaningful life is to make above-average contributions to the betterment of society (see also Matheson (2016, 82). Belliotti (2001, 73) rejects Baier's above-average theory on the grounds that it gives us reason to eliminate all humans who make more of a contribution than we do. Later in life Baier (1988, 47) seemed to relax his standards for meaning, holding that meaning cannot be subject to any "unfair gamble"; but then in the same piece he reasserts that meaning can depend on qualities like importance, which are hostage to fortune.

The Significance Impulse. Joshua Glasgow, Oxford University Press. © Oxford University Press 2024.
DOI: 10.1093/9780197754788.003.0005

70   THE SIGNIFICANCE IMPULSE

One last way of tying meaning to importance is weaker yet. On this account, being significant is not required for having a meaningful life. After all, couldn't you find meaning in some excellent activity even if it doesn't make you important?[3] But still, this third view says, doing significant things—making a big difference in the lives of others, having a sizeable impact, creating long-lasting value—can at least *add* substantial amounts of extra meaning that are not available in a merely ordinary life.[4]

All of these views converge, via their three unique paths, on the same rationale for the Significance Impulse: being important makes life more meaningful. But despite the widespread enthusiasm for this outlook, even here I think that Kahlo was right. Being important actually adds no meaning to our lives. To say this is not to say that significant accomplishments can have their meaning drained or overridden by a small but powerful incident elsewhere in life.[5] It's rather that importance does not add any meaning that might be overridden. Importance is not just unnecessary for meaning, it is downright irrelevant. Importance and meaning travel on different tracks.[6]

We should register up front that we are not likely to find a Grand Proof either in favor of or against there being a connection between importance and meaning in life. Instead, following a more workaday strategy, our argument here assembles real-world cases and thought experiments to support the claim that our importance does not, by itself, impact the meaning we draw from life. Although some

3. Schlick (2008).

4. Audi (2005); Baier (1988, 49); Belliotti (2001); Brogaard and Smith (2005, 445); Dworkin (2000, 252–253); Hooker (2008); James (2010); Kauppinen (2012); Levy (2005); Metz (2003, 66; 2013, 247); Persson and Savulescu (2019). See also Schmidtz (2002).

5. Morioka (2015, 54).

6. For other departures from the dominant consensus, see also Campbell and Nyholm (2015, 707–708); Rescher (1990, 161–162); Vitrano (2020); and Wolf (2014, 106).

readers will no doubt have diverging judgments about these cases, they at least demonstrate how we can plausibly explain the relevant dimensions of meaning in life without appealing to significance. The ultimate payoff is increased confidence both that we can find as much meaning in a merely ordinary life as we can find in an exceptionally important life and that being important does not in itself add any special meaning to the lives of important people.

How, then, might importance be linked to meaning in life? We have already seen one answer: the conjecture that, as a purely *semantic* matter, doing something meaningful by definition requires doing something important. To be sure, sometimes we do use the word "meaningful" in the sense of doing something "important" or "significant," such as when we talk about "making a meaningful contribution" as equivalent to "making an important contribution." But an equivocation lurks in these words: claiming that someone made a meaningful-qua-important contribution is not the same as claiming that having important lives, projects, or actions adds meaning-qua-prudential-value to those lives. The matter at issue between Williams and Kahlo is the extra-semantic question of whether being important in our sense also makes one's life more meaningful. And to make some headway on that issue, we need to know not whether the words "meaningful" and "important" can ever be used interchangeably but what adds meaning to our lives. This substantive question cannot be answered with a semantic stipulation. We instead must answer it with substantive evidence. The cases presented below are one bundle of such evidence.

* * *

Views on meaning in life are standardly divided into three camps. The first two, *pure subjectivism* and *pure objectivism*, are, I will argue, both flawed and when taken in isolation unhelpful for demonstrating that importance adds meaning to our lives; the third, a *hybrid*

72 THE SIGNIFICANCE IMPULSE

subjective–objective view, is more plausible, and its implications for being important are more complicated.

Start with purely subjectivist theories of meaning. Like subjectivist theories of *well-being*, subjectivist theories of *meaning* say, roughly, that doing what we *find* meaningful is all that it takes to add *actual* meaning to our lives.[7] On this way of looking at things, since Kahlo thought that importance does not add meaning to life, being significant did not pack any extra meaning into her life; but since Williams cared about being important, it did contribute meaning to his life. Significance is in his interests, but not hers, simply because he invested it with meaning while she did not. For subjectivists, that pretty much decides the question of whether we have any good reason to be important.

Clearly, doing important things sometimes seems to give people a feeling of satisfaction or fulfillment. But subjectivism is at bottom a theory of what makes life *actually meaningful*, not of what makes us *feel fulfilled*. As a result, subjectivism faces the well-documented problem of being incompatible with the fact that we sometimes make mistakes about what is meaningful. In saying this, it should be acknowledged that sophisticated subjectivism can account for many mistakes of meaning, by framing them as confusions about what *we ourselves judge* meaningful.[8] This powerful explanation capitalizes on the fact that we don't always know ourselves very well: *I thought I should spend all of my time and money on a new motorcycle, but now I understand that this wasn't what I truly judged meaningful.* But although ignorance of one's own self is one real source of mistakes about what makes life meaningful, still some other mistakes seem to be rooted not in gaps between what we mistakenly think we judge valuable and what we actually judge valuable but in discrepancies between what we *actually judge* valuable and what *actually*

---

7. More refined treatments of subjectivism about meaning in life can be found in Calhoun (2018, chap. 2); Luper (2014); Rowlands (2015); Singer (1992, 110); and Taylor (2008).

8. Calhoun (2018, 41).

MEANING 73

is valuable. It seems like we can wake up one day and realize that what really have been our genuine motivating reasons for acting were way off base. We were doing what we thought was meaningful, but our judgments were simply misguided: *I really did think that the motorcycle was the most meaningful part of my life, and wow, was I being stupid.* That phenomenon is what even sophisticated subjectivism cannot account for.[9]

Moreover, the nature of our discussion gives us an independent, dialectical reason to sideline subjectivism about meaning in life that is parallel to the dialectical reason we sidelined subjectivism about well-being in Chapter 4. Our question is whether we have any good reason to be important. The question itself is already grasping for something beyond the purely subjective that can *warrant* the preference for being important. This is what we are interrogating, the idea that being important is *worth* wanting. Is significance something we ought to seek for our lives—is there some reason to pursue it beyond the fact that we might want it? Who is *correct*, Kahlo or Williams? To have that conversation, we need to assume that there are some standards outside of the individual's own judgments about whether being important is meaningful; we need some external standards for assessing whether those judgments are well placed. (As we saw in Chapter 4, such external standards might be put in terms of mind-independent value, but also they might be rendered as a matter of intersubjective agreement or the values held by idealized versions of ourselves.) So in addition to the principled reason to reject pure subjectivism about meaning, also the very form of our question means that it must be answered outside the subjectivist's porthole. We're not asking what we *do* want for our lives. Again, we know that people do want to be important. Instead, we are asking what we *should* want for our lives. When that is the question, pure

---

9. For a rundown of many cases, from the harmful to the wasteful to the pointless, that have been used to show that people can make mistakes in subjectively judging things are meaningful when they in actuality are not meaningful, see Metz (2013, 175).

subjectivism is beside the point—except of course as grounds for rejecting the central, desire-evaluating question that animates our investigation.

The second theory of meaning in life is pure objectivism. This view states that what adds meaning to our lives is fixed by standards that receive no validation from our desires, preferences, or other subjective leanings. Instead, what gives our lives meaning is producing, finding, or instantiating purely *objective* value. Thus, Thaddeus Metz maintains that being subjectively drawn toward some endeavor is unnecessary for it to be meaningful. Mother Teresa's work was meaningful even if she was bored by it, Metz claims.[10] And others argue that important people like Mother Teresa, Einstein, and Gandhi had obviously meaningful lives precisely because of their special importance, regardless of their own subjective assessment of their works.[11]

Now because we can be drawn to what is objectively attractive, Cheshire Calhoun has noted an equally plausible *non*-objectivist explanation for why these figures led paradigmatically meaningful lives, an explanation that is open to both pure subjectivism and the third, hybrid view to be explored below: we suspect that these people found their work enormously engaging.[12] If we later discover that they were alienated from their work—as when we discovered that Mother Teresa experienced crises of faith—these cases buckle as paradigm cases of meaningful lives.

And as with pure subjectivism's struggle to make sense of mistaken judgments about the meaning of one's own projects, so too there are cases that tell against pure objectivism. Consider two dif-

---

10. Metz (2002, 797; 2003, 63; 2013, 183–184). Metz agrees that subjective engagement can *amplify* the meaning of a project, so it may not be fair to label him a pure objectivist. But he does hold that the subjective element is unnecessary and that objective impact can also increase meaning (2013, 247). His view might be best interpreted as a disjunctive thesis that meaning can be found in both purely objective ways and hybrid ways.

11. Bramble (2015, 452); Martela (2017, 244); cf. Smuts (2013).

12. Calhoun (2018, 40).

ferent kinds of crisis in meaning. The first comes from looking at your life and recognizing that you have been prioritizing the wrong things. The hedge fund manager retires at the age of fifty already worth a fortune, but it then dawns on him that having dedicated his entire adulthood to the pursuit of wealth, he neglected and ultimately became estranged from his partner, children, and friends. His life is not just lonely, which he knew for years; now he also rightly recognizes that a life full of money but empty of relationships is lacking in meaning. Objectivism (and hybridism, but not subjectivism) can capture this kind of crisis in meaning: the hedge fund manager failed to secure the things that objectively matter, or at least failed to secure them to the right degree and in the right way. By contrast, a second kind of crisis in meaning comes not from prioritizing projects that lack sufficient objective value; instead, the second crisis stems from prioritizing projects that you rightly recognize as valuable but that do not energize or excite or mobilize you.[13] Thus, John Stuart Mill famously discovered, not too far into adulthood, that his humanitarian goals left him rudderless. Though he judged his life's work immensely valuable, he still found himself in crisis: "[t]he end had ceased to charm," he wrote, "I seemed to have nothing left to live for."[14] This "burnout" kind of crisis stems not from securing the things that objectively matter—Mill's humanitarian *end* still was highly valuable, he thought—but from not being *moved by* one's own objectively valuable pursuits. Those important activities no longer "charmed" Mill. We need a theory that makes room for that second kind of crisis in meaning, and that requires meaning to have a subjective element.

Of course, pure objectivists have their cases, too, and one class of cases in particular may seem to justify seeking importance. Brad Hooker points us to someone who is a fantastic teacher, substantially improving the lives of his students, but who doesn't care about

13. Wolf (2010b, 21).

14. Mill (1971, 81).

76   THE SIGNIFICANCE IMPULSE

this work and in fact is disappointed at the end of his life that his teaching didn't serve what he really cared about, his research. If we wanted to console him on his deathbed, we might try to convince him that his teaching was meaningful by pointing to its impact. According to Hooker, this way of approaching our friend suggests that the objective value of teaching is sufficient to make the work meaningful, regardless of his subjective attraction to that work. In a similar vein, Bramble says that it makes sense to try to convince a depressed person that their life is meaningful by pointing exclusively to its objective value.[15] In these sorts of cases, if we can also point to a *lot* of objective value as making for *even more* meaning in these people's lives, then we could also conclude that being important adds extra meaning to one's life.

But a non-objectivist interpretation of these cases is also available, and in my estimation it is more compelling. When we call these people's attention to the objective value of these lives, the goal is not simply to prove to them that their lives are objectively valuable. Crucially, the depressed friend and the dying teacher could already agree that their lives have had objective value. After all, this is one way that depression manifests: as an inability to subjectively pursue, affirm, or take satisfaction from what one inertly judges objectively valuable. This means that, more than just getting our despondent friends to *acknowledge* the value in their lives, which might leave the despondency intact ("I know that my teaching added value to the world, but I just don't give a damn!"), we must also try to *engage* them subjectively with their lives' objective value. We want them to latch onto that objective value in a way that is powerful enough, affectively and motivationally, to help lift them out of their funk. We want them to *care* about that objective value, to find it *energizing.*

If I were disappointed to find myself unclogging septic lines for a living, you wouldn't have to convince me that this is valuable work. I agree that it is crucial, and I am glad that people do that

15. Hooker (2008, 193); Bramble (2015, 447).

work. What's more, despite my disappointment, I might even be contented living the plumb life: maybe I'm a happy-go-lucky person, maybe I'm loaded on uppers, or maybe I just enjoy listening to my co-workers' banter and podcasts all day. The problem remains, though, that I am still alienated from the work. Clearing septic lines is not a project that I find fulfilling or rewarding—it doesn't excite my emotions or mobilize me to action (I groan every day before work, doing it only for the paycheck). Consequently, my life has a hole that is ordinarily and aptly characterized as a lack of meaning.

How could you help me in that situation? I think the instinct that Bramble and Hooker's cases tap into is not that we want to convince despondent people that their lives have objective value. (Again, our despondent characters can already agree to that.) Rather, the thought behind help like the deathbed conversation is that attending to objective value can be a tool for getting us subjectively engaged. We hope that when the disappointed teacher fully appreciates the value in his accomplishments, he will *also* care about it. To find meaning people need not just to passively and coolly notice the value in what they are doing—a recognition that sometimes can manifest in affectless, motivationally silent ways, à la Mill—but also to let that knowledge color their lives.[16] If they can find the space to do that, then meaning will come rushing in.

(Here we come to a fork in the theoretical road. One path we could take says that when we newly care about some project that was always objectively valuable, but which we found uninspiring until now, it only has meaning from that point in time forward. Another path is that this newfound engagement retroactively revalues the entire project as meaningful, even before the newfound engagement kicked in; perhaps this is similar to how a sacrifice paying off can make the sacrifice meaningful. Both options are compatible with the views expressed here.)

---

16. Compare to Evers and van Smeden (2016, 360).

At our friend's deathbed we want to respect his predicament. We do not baldly invalidate his claim that his teaching has not added any meaning to his life. For him teaching is no more interesting than it would be for you to work on some project that you do not care about. Perhaps, if you are like me, it's clearing septic systems; or maybe you would be alienated from something else, like issuing people parking tickets or playing the sousaphone. When we find our lives filled with valuable activities that do not stir our passions, life can both feel and *be* empty of meaning. But when the task is not only objectively valuable but also engaging, what could have been a meaningless activity for us becomes meaningful.

Thus, the cases that might seem to support both pure objectivism and the claim that meaning increases with importance do not in fact support those views since the cases can also be equally well explained in these other ways. That said, in the event that you are not convinced to turn away from pure objectivism about meaning in life, note that even pure objectivists should question whether their view generates a rationale to value *importance*. Even if we only need objective value (and not also subjective engagement) to get meaning out of this life, why should we also add that the objective value must *escalate* to *increase* that meaning? Why can't the objective value of making lunch for some homeless people in your neighborhood be as meaning-giving as the more objectively valuable project of ending global hunger? There might be an answer to this escalation question—and we will give it an independent examination shortly—but merely being an objectivist about meaning in life is not enough to get all the way there: even if pro-importance objectivists can defend their objectivism, they would still need a further defense of the separate claim that producing *more* objective value generates *more* meaning in life. If we take the dispute between Williams and Kahlo seriously, then we cannot, on pain of assuming what needs proving, simply insist on such escalations of meaning.

So turn now to the third account of meaning in life. It departs from pure objectivism by retaining a starring role for the subjective,

MEANING

while also departing from pure subjectivism by carving out premium space for the objective, too. On this hybridist view, our lives gather meaning when we are subjectively drawn to, engaged in, and at least somewhat successful at pursuing projects that have objective value. In Susan Wolf's memorable slogan, we find meaning in life when subjective attraction meets objective attractiveness.[17] If collecting rainbow stickers provides you, subjectively, with plenty of felt fulfillment but lacks objective value, then collecting those stickers will not truly contribute any meaning to your life. And if cleaning out septic systems is objectively valuable but you aren't subjectively engaged in that project, then it too will not add meaning to your life. You need both ingredients, the subjective draw and the objective merits. And for most hybridists, you also need to be actively engaged in whatever is both subjectively and objectively attractive, and your pursuit of it needs to be at least moderately successful, in order for it to add meaning to your life.

Though I am a fan of the hybrid view of what can make life meaningful, it is a pretty short walk from hybridism to the conclusion that important activities add meaning to our lives. Making that connection just requires adding that missing premise from the pure objectivist, the premise that projects, pursuits, and relationships add increasing meaning to our lives as their objective value increases. After all, it does seem that the reason we *care* about meaning in life is that we want to connect our lives to some value outside of ourselves, and the way to *find* meaning is to invest in value outside of yourself—value that can be seen from outside of your own perspective.[18] Raise a kid, promote justice, set a record, run conduit

---

17. Wolf (2010b, 9). For a list of others who ally themselves with hybridism (to which I would add Belliotti 2001; Frankl 1959; and Landau 2017), see Metz (2013, 182 n. 1), who judges it "probably the most commonly held view period among contemporary philosophers who have thought about meaning in life."

18. Belliotti (2001); Darwall (1983, 165); Kitcher (2014, chap. 4); Landau (2017); Levy (2005); Metz (2013); Nozick (1981); Singer (1992, 1995); Wolf (2010a, 2014). See also Calhoun (2018, 25).

in a building, create beauty. Find yourself, or maybe lose your self, in monkish meditation. Live ethically. Love someone! These are the things that fill our lives with meaning, and the reason why seems to be that they have worth beyond what we merely find ourselves wanting to do—they bring their own value to the party. Notice that the external objective value we want to connect up with is not always limited to affecting *others* in a valuable way. On this construal of meaning's outside-in vector, although my achieving enlightenment helps me rather than others, it is nonetheless meaningful because whatever value enlightenment has lies outside of my merely choosing it. Meaningful goals might revolve around self-*focused* values, just not merely self-*created* values. As Hooker asks, if my life can get meaning from my positively impacting someone else, why can't it also get meaning from my positively impacting myself?[19]

What we want to know is: on the hybrid view, does it make a difference in meaning to go big with that external value—to end global hunger or to achieve enlightenment—or can meaning be equally secured by smaller value—buying a kid an ice cream cone or practicing some weekend mindfulness meditation? This is where many maintain that because connecting with objective value is what adds meaning to our lives, we should also say that connecting with *more* value makes life *more* meaningful. For example, Metz holds that the more impactful one's accomplishment, the more meaning it gives one's life. And Neil Levy writes that "the highest, most satisfying, kind of meaning" must involve open-ended projects "in which supremely valuable goods are at stake." This standard, for Levy, limits the meaning of routine activities such as raising kids or farming or investing in friendships. Those pursuits do generate a humdrum, ordinary meaning; but the bigger things in life, like doing philosophy, pursuing justice, and creating art, have the capacity to generate

---

19. Hooker (2008, 192); cf. Kitcher (2014, chap. 4); Metz (2013, 191–192); Wolf (2010b, 42; 2014).

MEANING   *81*

a special "superlative" meaning that Levy valorizes.[20] What these views have in common is what I will call the "escalation premise":

> *As a project or relationship or pursuit has more value, it adds more meaning to your life.*

Now recall one of the key elements in our analysis of importance, from Chapter 2:

> *Other things equal, to say that something is more important is to say that it has more value.*

Together the escalation and analytical premises justify the Significance Impulse: other things equal, the more important a project is, the more it adds meaning to your life. Since we have already seen good reason to accept the analytical premise, if this argument for the Significance Impulse goes astray, the source of the problem must lie with the escalation premise.

* * *

Let us change the trickster story from above. Imagine now that on your twenty-fifth birthday, he presents you with a choice that will determine how the rest of your life goes. One option is to have a life where you are a devoted parent, you enjoy a thriving and loving partnership, your career as a primary school teacher is fulfilling if unglamorous, and you are a fully integrated member of your local community. Like the pharmacist's life from the earlier story, this is the *ordinary* option. The alternative path is the same *extraordinary* option as before: you cure cancer. You can't have it both ways, for the trickster has been taken in by the view that truly great people "must organize their whole lives around a single enterprise. They must be monomaniacs, even megalomaniacs, about their pursuits."[21] So, the

---

20. Metz (2013, 247); Levy (2005, 177, 185). Levy's valuation of escalation is separate from his main claim, which is that open-ended projects are key to meaning.

21. Simonton (1994, 181).

trickster tells you, if you choose the extraordinary path, your work will mean that you have to move to a city where you don't know anyone, with no time for friends other than colleagues you see once in a rare while at conferences. Your life won't have the space for raising children or even maintaining a functional romantic partnership. And when you one day return to your hometown for your fiftieth high school reunion, your circle of childhood friends will remain close-knit, and you will be acutely aware of how distanced you have become from the people you once loved. But you would cure cancer.

Now add to this version of the story that you are the type of person who finds lab work painfully tedious. Worse still, the cancer-curing path requires a serial process of writing grants, supervising junior scientists, and managing a small bureaucracy that collectively would envelop your entire world in what for you is soul-crushing drudgery. It devastates you to think about spending the prime of your life drowning in pipettes and budgets. Compounding the problem even further, all that you really wanted out of life was to have a couple of children and be active in the small-town goings-on of Nowheresville. Your dream was to live on the same block as your childhood friends, raise kids alongside each other, grow old together, and reminisce on your front porches until the sun sets on a long, rich, connected life. This is what fulfills you, for better or worse. The trickster has presented you with this predicament: the life you really want for yourself will be the life you cannot have if you cure cancer; instead, you would end up living out one of the kinds of life that you most want to avoid.

As you deliberate, you concede that there are more overall points in favor of curing cancer than there are in favor of pursuing the ordinary life. Curing cancer is morally required, you recognize; and because of its immense value to humanity, it is probably rationally required overall. For the crucial fact added by the trickster in this version of the thought experiment (and unlike the earlier scenario with your neighbor) is that you are the *only* person who would cure cancer. Your situation is similar to that of many of the important people we admire, the Einsteins and Coltranes and Malalas and Huertas, where the scary possibility is that had they not acted as they did, perhaps nobody else would have either. There is no Leibniz to your Newton. So you conclude that you pretty much have to take the extraordinary path. But at the same time, that path feels like an incredibly burdensome obligation: because it would tear you away from what you most want for yourself and offer as a replacement unrelenting toil and chore, the extraordinary option has a much weaker grip on your motivational and emotional resources than does the possibility of spending your prime years living the ordinary life. And so, while being the one to cure cancer seems both rational and moral, one certain thing is that it would be a personal sacrifice. You judge this path a *worthwhile* sacrifice since you know it is the most choice-worthy choice you could make. And at times you will take some genuine satisfaction from all that you accomplish. Still, your life will seem much emptier than the life you could have had, where you would have been surrounded by engaging projects, laughing children, and the love of people close to you.

The problem in this scenario is not that you will be unhappy, for we can stipulate that on the extraordinary path you will see a fair amount of happiness: the pride, the adoration, the fine dinners ain't nothing, and anyway we can assume that you are the lucky type whose baseline happiness is stable at a relatively high level regardless of life circumstances. Rather the problem is that your life would have a massive hole in it. A profound sense of loss will persist even while you enjoy your cancer-curing life and proudly remind yourself that you have done work of tremendous, historic impersonal value. Looking around, some of your successful colleagues will seem different than you in this regard: monomaniacs that they are, they feel satisfied in their singular focus, while you know a bone-deep loneliness and a mixed but very real regret.

It is undeniable that the extraordinary path demands that you sacrifice; the question is how to characterize that sacrifice: Is it a sacrifice of well-being for meaning, or is it a sacrifice of meaning itself? Like many have said about Mill, my conjecture is that at least a good chunk of what you sacrifice on the extraordinary path is meaning—a kind of meaning onto which your fellow researchers seem to latch, while you struggle to connect to your venture. It is not merely that you would *think* the ordinary life would be more meaningful for you than the extraordinary life; it's that for you it would *be* more meaningful to parent children than to cure cancer. (Apparently for Mill the cure that restored meaning in his life was not having kids but instead reading poetry. Chalk up another score for experiments in living.) If you were to choose the extraordinary path, you would be important. You would do the right thing. You would even be happy to a degree. And still your life would lack meaning. This type of sacrifice is, for a certain kind of person, a real possibility.[22]

Other cases reinforce this judgment. Jerry Garcia destroyed himself through heroin because, some say, it offered relief from the relentless touring, which he kept up in order to keep his crew employed and Deadheads happy.[23] Assume for the sake of argument that he created objectively valuable art and helped sustain an objectively valuable social and creative movement. Still, that important work eventually became a poisonous burden for him. It apparently deprived his life of so much meaning that his only refuge was the hazy and eventually fatal cloud of a smack high.

---

22. Smuts (2018, 38) argues that in a similar case, curing cancer would not improve your *well-being* (leaving meaning aside). For an intuition that diverges from mine in a variation on the ordinary/extraordinary case, see Bramble (2015, 448), who interprets Mill as denying the value of his activities. By contrast (and with others such as Kekes [1986] and Sigrist [2015, 88–89]), I understand Mill, when he says that "the end had ceased to charm," as indicating that the end was still the *end*; that is, he still recognized it had value. Instead, it no longer had any purchase on his affective or motivational resources. R. W. Hepburn (1966, 128) puts this hybridist instinct nicely: "To seek meaning is not just a matter of seeking justification for one's policies, but of trying to discover how to organize one's vital resources and energies around these policies." This is what eluded Mill during his crisis.

23. Bar-Lev (2017).

A pair of familiar tropes cements the image: the executive who steps down from her demanding position at a world-changing charity in order to spend more time with the kids versus the alienated mother who wants to expand her horizons beyond homemaking in order to work with that world-changing charity. Both women find the charity work valuable. Both women also value their children and the project of rearing them in a loving, supportive home. And both women are, objectively, doing valuable things. But the lives that they have been leading equally lack meaning for them because each of the women is subjectively alienated from the way their lives are structured: they wish that they could trade places. Since it is possible for both lives to lack meaning equally, the fact that one of them is doing world-changing work while the other is doing ordinary work—the two women's differing levels of importance—appears not to be what is shaping the meaning in their lives.

These are all cases where we must trade one set of goods against *qualitatively* different goods: a rich home front versus profound professional possibilities, restoration for oneself versus joy or employment for many others, etc. Similar results emerge when we keep the kinds of goods in question identical and vary only their *quantity*. For instance, imagine now that you are a successful writer of popular history. You have won both riches and the admiration of your fellow historians. Your books have received prestigious awards and ecstatic reviews, and you have been rewarded with fancy jobs. As you plot out your next project, you come to realize that in these times the most impactful thing you could do is to write on demagoguery. However, you find that project uninspiring, boring, *obvious*, even though you have good reason to think that the public would eat it up and that (given your influence) it may in fact help nudge the world in a healthier direction. You'd rather write your next book on an obscure revolution in the textile industry. Your grandparents used to work in the Garment District, and when you were young they traded captivating stories as you played at their feet. So this project has more meaning for you, even though it is the less important project. Here too the intuitive verdict is, again, not just that you would *think* this is more meaningful but that you would be right: the less important project would *be* more meaningful for someone like you, with your particular background and proclivities.

The pattern also holds where the objective value at stake is not about impact on the *world* but instead is internal to *oneself*, such as cultivating one's own virtue or improving one's intellect or doing something creative. Say that I work on my fear of spiders rather than doing something more virtuous like developing my courage in battle, or I read a history book rather than getting a history Ph.D. Assume that the preferred activities all have *some* objective value, enriching the life of the person doing them, even though they have *less* objective value than the alternative projects. All the same, in these cases if our less objectively valuable option is more subjectively engaging, it will have more meaning for us. For people with a certain set of leanings, the more important alternative would be a *grind*.

Next, consider situations that combine value for oneself and impact on the world. Calhoun offers up a case of someone struggling to choose between becoming a biology professor and becoming a philosophy professor.[24] Even if these careers will equally contribute both to the world and to the person's intellectual development, that doesn't mean that they each would be equally meaningful pursuits for that person. Keeping all else equal, what would tip the scales is whatever area of study the person finds more interesting, more engaging.

These cases collectively reinforce the position shared by hybrid theory and subjectivism—but rejected by objectivism—that you must be attracted to a project or relationship for it to add meaning to your life. Moreover, to add to the already established hybridist picture of meaning in life, these cases suggest a novel specification that is key for our purposes: the *level* of subjective engagement,

24. Calhoun (2018, 24).

MEANING 87

the intensity of the project's grip on our motivational and affective resources, is what determines *how much* meaning the project or relationship adds to your life.[25] Conversely, increases in a project's objective value do not by themselves increase that project's meaning, contrary to the escalation premise. So having *some* objective value, on this hybrid account, is required for a project to give your life meaning. However, that is the only role objective value plays. Cranking up objective value past that minimal threshold, wherever it is, does not by itself add extra meaning to your life. Which in turn means that being important—being of exceptionally high value as opposed to being of more pedestrian value—does not by itself make your life more meaningful. What makes an above-threshold project more or less meaningful is the project being more or less subjectively engaging. And subjective engagement, of course, is available to the ordinary life as much as it is to the extraordinary life.[26]

As in other domains, it is tricky to identify exactly *where* the threshold is. (In keeping with the rest of the arguments made here, I suspect that to find the threshold we would need to tease the answer out of multiple cases that reside on the margins: Wolf is right that a lifetime full of passively watching sitcoms lies below the threshold, but a lifetime spent actively engaged in the theatrical arts lies above it; as we bring those lives closer together, where do we find a line of separation?) But we can settle other questions. One is why we should think that the threshold for sufficient objective value is low enough to encompass most ordinary lives. I think our

25. Though he is sometimes interpreted as an out-and-out subjectivist about meaning, it is plausible to read Harry Frankfurt (1999, 87) as advocating for something similar to this.

26. Calhoun (2018, 27–32) challenges hybrid conceptions of meaning on the grounds that they don't tell us how to balance the objective against the subjective. The view presented here meets that challenge by arguing for a simple answer: when it comes to meaning in life, once your pursuit or relationship or activity meets the minimum threshold of objective value, the level of subjective attraction does all the work of increasing or decreasing meaning.

intuitions about the above cases, such as the two mothers, require us to say that.

A harder question is why we should think that meaning in life is sensitive enough to objective value that it requires a minimal threshold of objective value but not so sensitive as to escalate with increasing objective value above the threshold. Here is one answer. Paradigm cases of meaning*less* lives are cases where the persons living them are *wasting* their lives, whether that be because they only do pointless tasks (like Sisyphus)[27] or they are confined to a closed loop of activities that feed each other[28] or they only pursue seemingly stupid projects like counting blades of grass or passively watching sitcoms for their entire lives.[29] Thus, there is an independent motivation for the threshold: for a project to be meaningful, it must not be a waste. It must participate in some amount of genuine value. But there is no such independent motivation for the escalation premise. And again, we have seen reason to doubt it: intuitively, ample supplies of meaning can be found in raising a child or writing a new song. To justify the escalation premise, the burden lies on the pro-importance crowd to show how it affects the amount of meaning we extract from life whether that child turns out to be Mother Teresa or the new song is "Let It Be."

Of course, we are often subjectively attracted to what is objectively attractive. We dream of doing important things—curing cancer, stabilizing the climate, writing "Let It Be"—precisely because the important things have outsized objective merits. Objective value can fuel subjective engagement, and arguably there is some rational pressure to align our subjective engagements with objective value, though surely that pressure is defeasible, too. This, I suspect, may go some distance to explaining why so many have been

27. Taylor (2008).

28. Levy (2005); Nozick (1981); Wiggins (1976).

29. Wolf (2010a).

attracted to the escalation premise: they take note of the fact that we are rationally attracted to doing important things. (Another driver of the error, I suspect, is the equivocation noted earlier, that "meaningful" can be used to refer to one aspect of prudential value and, separately, to refer to the size of a contribution.) But objective value is not the only determinant—not even the only *rational* determinant—of what we find ourselves attracted to. We are often rightly engaged in our pursuits and our relationships because of various contingencies of the self: our culture, our upbringing, our material and social conditions and opportunities, our idiosyncratic experiences, our individual biological makeup. Consequently, the subjective and the objective can cleave apart. When this happens, as in the cases we have looked at, it makes sense to hold that, above the minimal threshold of objective value, what determines how much meaning we secure is the subjective part, not the objective part—not whether our projects are extraordinarily important.

This central role of subjective contingencies in determining what gives our lives meaning raises another question: Does the causal source of our subjective attractions matter? If we can derive meaning from projects in a way that is partly due to a variety of subjective pathways, can we purposefully engineer those pathways to increase our meaning in life? There are certain ways that this might seem less valuable, such as if you took a drug to increase your interest in nature, so that you spend less time watching sitcoms and more time exploring the natural world, rather than organically making that change.

Our version of hybridism is compatible with any answer to this question. We might say, for example, that since it would not diminish the meaning of Coltrane's creations or Malala's activism if they had to cultivate the interests that led to their achievements, so engineering subjective attraction does not diminish the meaning of more ordinary pursuits, either. Or perhaps there ought to be some limits on how the cultivation happens. Maybe certain subjective attractions are more *authentic* if they stem from years of work, say, than if they stem from taking a drug. Or maybe not. If someone is struggling because their alcoholism is dampening their subjective attraction to their family life, and if they take a drug to counteract that alcoholism, and if that results in more attraction to family life, then that hardly seems like an inauthentic source of meaning. In any event, again, while more work would need to be done to identify the shape of such restrictions on meaning, we can rest assured that any restrictions along those lines are adaptable to the kind of hybrid, no-escalation view being advanced here.

That said, this argument is still incomplete. Against the escalation premise, our cases so far suggest that the level of our subjective attraction, rather than the level of (supra-threshold) objective value, is what determines how much meaning in life we get. But all the case-pairs so far used feature different levels of subjective attraction. So we still need to know what happens if we hold subjective attraction steady and only vary levels of objective value. In cases where we face two paths that are equally subjectively attractive, if one path is much more objectively valuable than the other (and if both are above the minimum threshold), wouldn't you choose the more important path? Couldn't significance at least function as a tie-breaker?

If I faced this kind of choice, I would choose the more important path. But though it would be the more *choice-worthy* path, I do not think it would add more *meaning* to my life. Its increased objective value provides it with no additional meaning for me than would increasing the importance of some project that I have *no* subjective attraction to, such as if you moved my job cleaning septic systems from a gated community of expensive vacation homes to an impoverished city that is knee-deep in a sanitation crisis. Unless, that is, I start to find that more important project more motivationally and affectively engaging—perhaps I become moved by its enlarged objective value—in which case this newfound portion of subjective engagement would carry with it an emergent dose of surplus meaning.

This verdict also seems plausible if we instead *decrease* objective value while subjective attraction remains stably elevated. Imagine, for example, a less valuable version of an important artist or scientist: they are as engaged in their art or science just as much as their superstar counterpart, but their work is less significant. My intuition, and I suspect the intuition of many who occupy an egalitarian, come-as-you-are approach to prudential value, is that the less important (but still above-the-threshold) career makes for as meaningful a life as is had by the person with the more important career.

A similar scenario features a trade-off between a little more subjective value and a *lot* more objective value. Consider the immense objective value of curing cancer versus the comparatively low-value endeavor of making pizza for hungry pizza lovers. Can I really devote myself to making pizza instead of curing cancer, if I am the only one available to perform either task and I cannot do both of them?

Most of us would rather cure cancer than make pizza—our subjective attraction aligns with objective attractiveness in this case. But if your tastes are different, the apron may offer more meaning than the lab coat. Even if curing cancer is what you have most overall reason to do, and even if you are moderately attracted to it, it may not be what fills your life with meaning if you find yourself significantly more attracted to a different life choice. There is abundant evidence for the intuitiveness of this assessment: while nobody I know would choose to make pizza instead of curing cancer, every single person I know makes a lower-stakes version of that trade-off on a routine basis. Instead of doing something noble and important, we hang out with friends. We watch our favorite team in the big game. We play some music. Pleasure and morality are not the only values hanging in the balance here; these ordinary pursuits and relationships are the staples that nourish our lives with meaning, too.

And so it is reasonable to provisionally conclude that the escalation premise sits on quicksand. Like Mill, if you try to end poverty—even if you *succeed*—you could find your life dulled in meaning even as it shimmers in significance. And if instead, like almost everyone else, you just try to live a decent regular life, then your import will dwindle but you might still enjoy a life rich in meaning.

6

The Significance of Insignificance

On a clear night and with a wide view, taking in some of the tinsel strewn across the black sky, it is easy to be struck by the idea that all that is out there is you and a handful of other conscious creatures tumbling through a purposeless and mostly empty field. In that thought, our fragility underwrites a peculiar terror: we are potentially the only sources of feeling and thinking, and soon enough all of humanity will be recaptured by the void, too, decayed and granulated and scattered to the eternity that contained our burst of significance within a sliver of a shred of a fragment of time and space.

It is only one step from that predicament to the one that has occupied us in this book: the cosmic prank is that even we are not that important. True enough, when the stardust is whirled together into humanity's conscious, agential, playful, purposive, self-reflective nobility, value emerges. But still, cosmically speaking, this value is relatively modest. We totter around our small garden off to the side of the universe, seeking a snack and some shelter and, on the good days, a pursuit worth pursuing. We can barely contribute what matters, even assuming that what matters most is our consciousness or our love. Even assuming that, among all the extant objects in

The Significance Impulse. Joshua Glasgow, Oxford University Press. © Oxford University Press 2024.
DOI: 10.1093/9780197754788.003.0006

the universe, what matters most is us, we still lack cosmic levels of significance.

This cosmic insignificance has been a fertile soil for panic and discouragement. Crushed by the sage's argument, Blaise Pascal wrote, "[w]hen I consider the short duration of my life, swallowed up in an eternity before and after, the little space I fill, and even can see, engulfed in the infinite immensity of spaces of which I am ignorant, and which know me not, I am frightened."[1] The most popular way to grapple with that fear is to fight its starting premise and insist that we are in fact significant, after all. Ronald Dworkin, for example, writes that if we just live well, we transform from mere "blinks of duration" into "tiny diamonds in the cosmic sands."[2] But as exciting as that prospect sounds, we have seen how even our best roles are more prosaic. We do put understanding and love and good works into the emptiness of the universe. But for all our well-lived lives, we are not cosmic diamonds. From the widest angle, someone who saves a life, or who creates something wonderful, or who leads some people away from pain is a fraction more luminous than the ordinary person; but even the heroic humans could have been so much more important than they are. Cosmically speaking, we are all, each and every one of us, cubic zirconium.

Others fight off pessimism by maintaining that making a difference to one person is not more important than impacting the lives of billions.[3] But while this book has agreed that the size of one's impact is unnecessary for living a life that is flush with meaning and well-being, we have also seen that, as a conceptual matter, impact can determine how *important* a person is. At least, it can if we are going to talk about these things in a way that latches onto importance in the sense operative here, the sense that excites Ted

---

1. Pascal (1958, sec. 205)

2. Dworkin (2013, 423).

3. Kitcher (2014, 109).

THE SIGNIFICANCE OF INSIGNIFICANCE   95

Williams' enthusiasm and Frida Kahlo's derision. In our sense, being significant requires having truly extraordinary value, and so being cosmically important would require cosmically extraordinary value.

Instead of grasping for a status that is out of our reach or redefining what counts as important, a more promising salve for Pascalian pessimism emerges out of our last two chapters: fear is misplaced for those with little significance. You would not have benefited by being extraordinarily significant, anyway. You might have a *moral* obligation to do the important things that are within your power, and if you are the only one who can do something great for the world, then arguably there is *impersonal* value to your being globally important in that way. You may well even have *personal* reasons to achieve what you can, to flourish internally, and to grab any rewards that society attaches to more important pursuits. But just in terms of your own personal interests, being cosmically great would not by itself add any value to your own life. It would not have packed your life with extra meaning, and it would not have made you better off than more pedestrian achievements or efforts would. From the perspective of self-interest, importance is unimportant.

Next, we take one final step in the march against pessimism, by finding a positive reason for full-throttle optimism: Is it possible that being unimportant is not only *not bad* but downright *good* for us?

* * *

Different kinds of pessimism call for different responses. For example, Arthur Schopenhauer thought that we are essentially strivers, and so we are doomed either to frustration at not reaching whatever we are striving for or to boredom once we have reached the endpoint of those strivings.[4] Schopenhauer's dilemma, if on point,

---

4. Schopenhauer (2004). It appears that Schopenhauer did not appreciate that the journey, or the activity itself, can have value (Setiya 2014).

96   THE SIGNIFICANCE IMPULSE

would apply to strivers like us whether or not we are important. And any ways that we might deal with being buffeted between boredom and frustration will provide no relief for Pascal's kind of pessimism, which is specifically directed at our cosmic insignificance.

A different and for our purposes more instructive basis for pessimism looms closer to Pascal's concern about being insignificant: the nihilistic worry that we cannot find a justification to think that the world has any value at all. Recall that if nihilism is right, then we have no reason to think that we or anything else could be important, because if we have no reason to think that anything has *any* value, then we also have no reason to think that anything has *rare and high* value. But more than that, on this kind of nihilism that denies all value, all our beliefs and choices are completely unjustifiable, which threatens not just the important things, or even all that we care about; it is a threat to caring itself. Why care if you cannot have any reason to care?

Because of that threat, Albert Camus feared that giving up the belief that the universe contains value may lead some people toward suicidal ideation. To stave off that disaster, Camus championed defiance, insisting on a value-laden world regardless of where the evidence takes us. Finding this attempt at rescuing value from the clutches of nihilism "romantic, and slightly self-pitying," Nagel settles instead for irony, casually accepting the incongruity that we must go about our lives as if we matter, while being simultaneously sentenced to know deep down that, from an objective standpoint, we have no good reason to think that we or anything else matter at all.[5]

Perhaps I should be more ironic about this, but wholly suspending my commitment to objective values and reasons for both caring and acting is something I find intolerable. For although I have been lucky, I have also suffered and seen people I care about suffer, and I cannot get around the impression that this suffering is bad and

5. Camus (2008); Nagel (1971, 726); cf. Feinberg (2008).

that we have good reason to avoid suffering. The same impression of value seems to give us reason to foster joy, too. Once one occupies this value-embracing stance, justified or not, one relinquishes the option to take either the nihilistic or the ironic stance. When in the value-engaged perspective, I cannot keep in my head the distinct thought that what one most cares about is not worth caring about; and similarly, when I try to adopt the detached perspective that objectively there is no true value in the universe, I lose any subjective drive, including, importantly, the drive to irony. And I cannot find any space between the two perspectives. Detached irony is unavailable to the self-aware valuer.

This is where we find something unstable about recommending that we take an ironic stance toward the supposed lack of any rational support for belief in objective value. Nagel's reason for skepticism about objective value is based in the argument that all of our choices appear to be, objectively speaking, arbitrary. Roughly, the idea is that objectively we know that we cannot find a justified, non-arbitrary foundational value from which all other value is justified because that justifying value itself would have to be justified by reference to some further value, which means that the justifying value is not actually a foundational value after all. In this way, we are aware that objectively justified values must elude our grasp. And yet we also cannot escape, subjectively, the value-embracing orientation within which we live, where we seek well-founded justifications for our choices. Thus, Nagel thinks we are stuck with ironic acceptance of our mutually incompatible objective and subjective standpoints.[6] But if the objective stance insists that *no* choice is truly commendable, then it cannot make sense to *recommend* any choice—be it resignation, desperation, defiance, enthusiasm, or even Nagel's irony. No choice, nor anything else, carries with it any commendation, warrant, rationality, or value, on this way of look-

---

6. For more on this way of framing it, also see Nagel (1986).

ing at things. No attitude, irony included, can be deemed justifiable if we give up our commitment to justification.

Instead, truly suspending one's belief in value at best seems to leave choosers like us with what Nagel hopes we can avoid: paralysis of the will. How would you choose between two options, if you believed that there is no reason at all to favor any option at all? Similarly, Camus should not have been worried that nihilistically rejecting value could lead some agents to valorize nonexistence because an evaluation like that requires the agent to make the value judgment that nonexistence would be better than existence—exactly the kind of judgment that is unavailable within nihilism. A world where we do not recognize value is a world where we do not think we have justification for *any* choice, including the choice to live or die. If Schopenhauer's dilemma depicts us as insatiable complainers, Nagel and Camus' corner seems to paint us as Buridan's ass, where our fate is the inability to choose anything.

But even without a proof of objective value, there is a way to avoid paralysis of the will. Moreover, this path away from pessimism can also point us to a benefit of being only of minor importance. It takes the form of what we might call a "bizarro dilemma," a pair of options where both paths are *wins*, rather than losses as in normal dilemmas. It centers on what attitude we should take toward our choices. On the one hand, assume that our drive to believe in value and justified choice is correct and the nihilistic idea that all our choices are objectively unjustifiable is actually incorrect. In that case, there is some objective, external justification for certain choices being wise and others unwise. Perhaps that justification eludes us, but still good and right choices would exist, on this first option. We would be right to live our lives on the supposition that things matter, offering us the starting point we need in order to care about things sensibly. Win number one.

On the other hand, assume now that objectively speaking the nihilist is right that no choice can be justified by reference to objective values; our drive to objectively justify what we do is a distor-

THE SIGNIFICANCE OF INSIGNIFICANCE 99

tion, an error. In that case, then one implication is that we need not fret about it. On this second path, fretting is never justified because *nothing* is justified. In that respect, the absence of objective value liberates us to pursue whatever we want. This is win number two. Of course, we would be unable say that this liberation is a *good* thing since on this second tine of the fork there are no good things, nor any bad things. But still, it would probably feel pretty pleasant to not have to worry about living up to *objective external standards of rational choice*. Compare how a youngish adult feels upon realizing that they no longer need to satisfy the standards set by their parents. There might be an existential moment of unmoored nausea, but eventually they discover that they like the independence from those externally imposed standards. In a similar manner, even a *complete* absence of value need not paralyze your will. Instead, while we would not be justified in taking an ironic or any other stance— again, no justification of any kind is available on this second horn of the bizarro dilemma—the total absence of value would at least liberate you to follow your desires without having any reason to worry that your desires are errant (nor any reason to aspire to their correctness).

In short, if the nihilist is right that there is no value, then at least we can rest assured that we might enjoy the freedom to stop worrying about justifying our choices. That result has something to teach us, too, when we re-establish our starting assumption that there is value (in deference to the Significance Impulse) and try to resist Pascal's non-nihilistic but pessimistic premise that our having relatively *little* value is also a fearsome state of affairs.

* * *

Consider the often-celebrated perspective of Edgar D. Mitchell, lunar module pilot for the Apollo 14 landing mission:

100   THE SIGNIFICANCE IMPULSE

> In outer space you develop an instant global consciousness, a people orientation, an intense dissatisfaction with the state of the world, and a compulsion to do something about it. From out there on the moon, international politics look so petty. You want to grab a politician by the scruff of the neck and drag him a quarter of a million miles out and say, "Look at that, you son of a bitch."[7]

Getting perspective on one's own cosmic insignificance inspires an earnestness of purpose that is evoked in Mitchell's humbling experience. Rather than meeting our smallness with fear or fist-shaking, he finds himself with a sincere *embrace* of the cosmically small value of earthly things. Recognition of our cosmic mediocrity allows Mitchell to refocus his awareness on the bigger value puzzle, one that shows the politician's concerns to be petty. Instead of reaching for humanity to acquire more and more cosmic value, we accept, in our smallness, permission to pursue the smaller things, to chase only what is of limited significance right here in the tiny nursery in which we briefly make our home, and to see the silliness in being power-hungry about that little value that we get to enjoy. In these short lives of ours, we have room to create love and be decent to people. We can experience a stunning concert. We can wonder, in our weakness, at planet-smashing forces. As long as we do not matter so much, we should go ahead and walk in the woods or think through a puzzle or solve a problem. Help someone. Laugh out loud. That all becomes *easier* if we do not matter very much.

Consider what it would look like to be more important. For example, it would have dramatic implications for our moral duties, and thus for the quality of our lives.[8] If we had more power, size, or duration, our greater abilities would place us under more strenu-

---

7. "Edgar Mitchell's Strange Voyage," 1974.

8. For fuller articulation of this argument, see Wolf (1982) and Smilansky (2012), where one can find an extensive catalog of the downsides of the moral pressure to make an outsize difference.

THE SIGNIFICANCE OF INSIGNIFICANCE   *101*

ous moral obligations to do more, in what Saul Smilansky calls the "Super-person Paradox." Whatever freedom we currently have to pursue our own individual goals, it would be ever more dominated by bigger powers to make a huge difference. We would lose all moral latitude to goof off, if we were constantly running around saving the universe. We would be very boring people, too. You would lack any willingness for playfulness when you find yourself drowning in a sea of sensitivities and enjoy no free time for personally satisfying projects. Basic pleasures like laughter and sex are going to be on a serious diet while you are fighting bad guys, floods, and germs. One of the truest bits of philosophy ever penned was, "I find a world without beer too grim to contemplate."[9] If being cosmically important means no time for beer, well, then prudence counsels us to decline the laurels of cosmic significance.

Our project is not to catalog the ways that moral demands can stifle us, nor to prognosticate how our moral interests would stifle us even more if we were more powerful than we currently are. Rather, we can focus our exploration on a parallel point that is limited to our own *self-interest*. Mitchell found that our small lives offer us earnest celebration of the mundane. That is the purely personal benefit of bathing in mid-level value that we would lose if we were more extraordinary. If our cosmically importance mattered to our personal interests, then just as we would have to make more sacrifices for the greater good, we would be under correspondingly more prudential pressure to make sure that all of our personal choices are the right ones, too. The more important you are, the higher the stakes in everything you do. By contrast, as long as we remain relatively insignificant, we and the world around us matter enough (we go on assuming) to bother caring about, but not so much that we need to take ourselves too seriously. This is good news because taking oneself lightly can be its own virtue.[10] What survives the clash between being garbage and being the most valuable thing is weightier

9. Sher (2003, 33).

10. Bell (2019).

than pure nothingness but lighter than the pretentious strut of cosmic-grade ambition. If we take our value exactly as seriously as it demands, what we both can and ought to do is attend to the pain and suffering and peace and ecstasy of those with equally insignificant lives, to the beauty of our landscapes and our art, to the poignancy in our relationships, to the way things work and the ways we can remake our world without destroying the meager value that it contains. In other words, we can live perfectly normal human lives without apology. Instead of fear or surrender, on the one hand, and instead of the pompous pride of cosmic-scale aspirations, on the other, what the human condition really warrants is *irreverent contentment*.

When we are in the grip of the Significance Impulse, we hubristically envision fantasy versions of ourselves: How great can we be? What is our limit? Is galaxy-conquering power or immortality a possibility? When we challenge the Impulse, this fantasy looks both naïve and silly, and the only reasonable reaction is irreverence, putting the politicians inside all of us back in their places. Earnest acceptance of our insignificance affords us a less entitled (and less ridiculous) stance, one lying closer to the perspective of gratitude. In this stance we compare our lot not with how things could be *grander* but with how much *worse* things could have been: there could have been no us, we could have had more miserable lives, we could have been replaced by less valuable versions of ourselves, we could have mattered not at all. Rather than grasping for cosmic importance, this appreciative, contented pose smacks of a healthy realism.[11]

Jon Stewart once characterized satire as "comedy about things you care deeply about."[12] Satire does not say that the target of the joke does not matter. Nobody ever delivered a punchline about dust. Instead, you laugh at the politician who takes themselves so seriously, both because they are not as important as they think they

---

11. For more on contentment and gratitude, see Calhoun (2018, chap. 7) and Glasgow (2020).

12. Bateman, Hayes, and Arnett (2021).

THE SIGNIFICANCE OF INSIGNIFICANCE   *103*

are *and* because they are important enough to be worth our attention. Satire says that the butt of the joke does matter but also that there is a ceiling to that value: don't take yourself so seriously. As in its idiom of satire, inhabiting the space of irreverence allows us that more apt pose. It unveils the way in which Pascalian terror does not make sense: to be small is not to have anything special to be afraid of; it is only to be small.

That said, deflating the Significance Impulse invites a new risk: we might be *so* playful about the little value we sprinkle onto the world that we don't take serious concerns seriously enough. For example, it might seem to invite history's madmen to consider their cosmic unimportance and conclude, "Well, we don't matter too much, nor does anyone else, so that whole genocide thing is no big deal." Does taking up an irreverent stance toward humanity create room for people to do *anything*?[13]

No, it does not. As in satire, irreverence still recognizes value (while keeping it in its proper perspective), and even if we're just scratching the surface of our little rock, we still have value and thus demand ample responsibility from others. The fact that Americans don't matter very much on a cosmic scale does not give Canadians the right to colonize us. For one thing, Canadians don't matter any more than the rest of us do (sorry!). More crucially, relatively unimportant people still enjoy the protection of moral status. To say we are cosmically unimportant is not to rob us of that standing. The imperative to be moral holds steady regardless of whether the people you affect are extraordinary or merely ordinary. Our cosmic unimportance cuts us down to size in terms of the value we contribute to the universe, but it does not mean that morality, or logic, or wisdom changes. It does not mean that crimes are no longer criminal. And morality aside, little value is still value, and it must be taken care of exactly in proportion to its value.[14] To not care at all would

---

13. Compare Jollimore (2020, 54). I am grateful to Lucia Schwarz for pushing me on this question.

14. Compare Landau (2017, 86, 94–95).

be the most tragic way to live if there is even just one drop of value in the universe.[15] So being small is being small; it is not the same as being of zero value, and morality constrains our actions as long as they affect that which has value. Mattering a little bit is far from being cosmically important, but that is a difference of *degrees*; by contrast, mattering a little bit, and in particular mattering morally, gets you an entirely different *kind* of status than mattering not at all.

The real danger comes not from cosmic humility but instead from two other sources. One is the kind of nihilism that removes all value and thereby licenses any behavior whatsoever. The other danger comes from those whose misguided aspirations to being important lead them to conclude that they must stack humanity's morally equal zirconia into hierarchical pyramids, where the view from the top is nice but the structure crushes those at the base. Those who are under the spell of the Significance Impulse not only face the problem that their quarry will always be elusive—though it will be. Worse, people who seek to boost their own importance often seem tempted to use or destroy other people who stand in the way of that project. The Significance Impulse is one of those cognitive distortions that can steer the errant toward hurting others. In this way, the bigger threat to humanity is not rejecting the Impulse but giving into it. This seems to be what Mitchell saw.

But enough about risk to humanity; let us return to our own self-interest! The ultimate payoff to your personal well-being of being unimportant is that wonderful, delightful liberation where the irreverent always find their home. Pascal's fear misses the fact that if nothing in your life matters too much, then you are warranted to take it easy to the same degree. We still must respect moral constraints; otherwise, go ahead and enjoy the ride and not take your situation so seriously. And that is how our cosmic unimportance is not something we should feel *resigned* to. We can *revel* in it. Just like our liberated reaction to nihilism, where the complete absence of

15. Kahane (2017).

THE SIGNIFICANCE OF INSIGNIFICANCE   *105*

value at least means that we do not need to worry about what we do, so too the fact that our choices only matter a little bit, cosmically speaking, can give us a beneficial kind of freedom.

Though there is said to be a kind of freedom in aligning your cares and your actions,[16] there is another kind of freedom that stems from putting your cares in their own box. Consider the drive to see one's achievements ripple across the fabric of the universe. Many people can probably relate to Horace, Tolstoy, and Velleman's (and others') hope that their works will still be read in a million years. What is less often remarked on is how nobody says that sort of thing about their failures. Nobody desires that in a million years people are still learning about the time you hurt your friend's feelings or that aliens in distant galaxies might study the episode when your big idea at work proved to be a disaster. We want our weaknesses to sink to the bottom of the ocean, our mistakes to disappear before their consequences are fully realized, our loss and suffering to just go away. This is where cosmic insignificance can supply a relief valve for the misguided pressure, explored in the previous chapter, of trying to optimize one's connection to positive value: if we do not matter all that much, then while all our achievements might not count for very much, neither do life's disappointments. Our failures, our flaws, our inaction, our pain matter still, but only to that same limited degree.[17]

The freedom at play in irreverence is not the freedom of being uncoerced by another, nor freedom from the government or any other social power telling you what to do. It is not the freedom of autonomy, and it is not free will. It is, instead, freedom from the unrelenting insistence that we must make good choices. It is freedom from the tyranny of value. When we take ourselves seriously, we worry about whether this is the right year to have kids, or whether to have them at all. Whether this is the right college major,

16. Frankfurt (1988).

17. Compare Singer (1992, 124).

or whether to go to college at all. Whether the best path in life takes you around the world or just around town. Whether we should pay for this or for that. Hell, the lucky ones sometimes agonize over what to eat for dinner. Our cosmic unimportance secures a degree of relief from these pressures that we put on ourselves: when things don't matter so much, we don't have to care so much about optimizing. Little enough is at stake that we do not need to care, let alone feel bad, when we fail in our effort to get the right answers to life's questions. The poor choice turns out to be not so regrettable, even though it remains a poor choice. Irreverence gives you a green light to laugh at your errors and move on. Our insignificance makes it rational to not care too much about being rational.

One reason we like playing games is that they transport us to a world where we can get lost in pretending that what does not really matter does matter. Can I get the ball to its target? Can I roll a different number on the dice? Can I find the most advantageous space for my little knight? That pretense frees us for a while from our real-life worries.[18] Stressed out about work, or your parents, or politics? Then pick up a ball, shuffle the deck, set up the board. It is the same escapism found in a good novel or movie: to leave your troubles behind, immerse yourself in a fictional world where it only *seems* like something important is at stake, where you temporarily invest enough in a made-up drama that you care but not so much that it has real consequences for the value in the world. When we escape in these ways what we are freed from is the weight of being concerned with *truly serious things*. That is freedom from the tyranny of value. It is a relief, even a *joy*, to enter these flatter worlds of make-believe. While we may become invested in the game's outcome, it stays recreational as long as somewhere we remember that it doesn't really matter all that much.

The freedom on offer by being unimportant is the freedom to extend that carefree attitude to a greater range of our pursuits,

18. Scheffler (2013, 58).

THE SIGNIFICANCE OF INSIGNIFICANCE 107

beyond our made-up worlds of play and fiction and into the rest of our lives. This freedom is not quite as liberating as a game you can just walk away from because (we continue to assume, contrary to nihilism) you and your pursuits do still truly matter: if there is value in the universe, then the kind of human life we are warranted in pursuing is more constrained than a made-up game where valuelessness is pretended to be valuable. Unlike a game where you are supposed to dominate or lie or cheat or destroy, in real life hurting a person still looks like hurting a person, and morality has something to say about that. But life does become more game-like to the extent that aspiration for cosmic importance converts into a playful attitude toward how much you and your pursuits matter. From the cosmic perspective, when we realize that our world doesn't matter *so, so much*, we can better enjoy life for the modest value that it promises.

A large chunk of humanity—academic researchers and self-help authors, priests and counselors, novelists and songwriters, policy-makers and educators—has invested serious resources in trying to help us think right and make sound, healthy decisions. I do not doubt that this project makes sense. However, if it is wise to not care too much about the decisions we make, then we can also rationally contain the always-looming expectation to make rational choices. Given that we matter, you still have to care about what choice you make; but given that we do not matter too much, you do not have to care too much about getting that choice just right. You still get to love what you love; you just don't have to think that your love, or your pain, or the love and pain of those around you is everything. Freedom from the tyranny of value is liberation by degrees from the pressure of the pros and the concern of the cons.

To be sure, this is not the idea that it can sometimes be rational to aim at what is suboptimal.[19] The irreverent stance does not generate a standard for selecting the right item on the menu; it is not a theory of rational choice. Instead, the irreverent stance is a perspective on

19. For that distinct idea, see Slote (1989).

the entire menu, an attitude we take toward whatever standards should ultimately govern our choice of its items. This meta-attitude applies *regardless* of what item on the menu we ought to choose—that is, independently of both the choice that we *believe* is rational and the choice that *actually* is most rational. Rather than offering a theory of what is rational, good, or right, the irreverent stance insists that there are limits to how much we should care about what is rational, good, or right. It is a rationally solicited gestalt shift. When we properly "get some perspective" or "take the long view" or "look at the big picture," our failures become less remarkable, and anxiety over our choices looks out of place or, worse yet, self-absorbed. The freedom at stake here is the freedom of knowing that there are limits to how much you should care about which path you do choose and which path you *should* choose, when it comes time to make a decision. In this, our post-ironic age of anxiety, freedom from the tyranny of value is the upside of being insignificant.

Thus, whereas someone like Camus might think that our best freedom lies in getting to assert objective value regardless of the evidence, I think that our best freedom lies in not worrying too much about how well we lash our choices to objective value—while also still caring enough to at least try to make the right choice. At the same time, we ought not get carried away by this good news. This liberation has limits that go beyond just the constraints of morality. They stem from the fact that the cosmic scope is only one frame of reference for evaluating ourselves. From other perspectives, at other scales of concern—when evaluating our lives in other *contexts*—we have other levels of significance that can render us less free. Most obviously, we are tremendously important to those in our social networks even though we are not very important to the universe, and so while we do not need to worry about our place in the cosmos, we still may need to worry about our place in our communities. But still, while our local import genuinely cranks up the stakes on our choices, the cosmically irreverent person recognizes that any fitting concern about our choices must be locally contained, too,

THE SIGNIFICANCE OF INSIGNIFICANCE   *109*

and can be counterbalanced with cosmic lightheartedness. It can be comforting to know that even though you screwed up, it does not matter *so, so* much. That knowledge justifiably liberates us to pursue our little worlds with more joy and comfort, enabling us to live better lives than we would be justified in living if we instead had to aspire to cosmic importance, too.

Pascal is hardly the only one to freak out at the thought that we are little more than stardust; fears of cosmic insignificance seem to have a terrible grip on people's sense of self-worth.[20] The Significance Impulse is powerful, as manifested not only by would-be messiahs, world conquerors, and hoarders of wealth and power but also in routine attempts to leave lasting legacies or create eternal works of art or engineering. Succumbing to such pressure leaves little room to maneuver and much to worry about. Irreverence is the escape vehicle to climb in when we are ready to elude those misvalued traps of ambition.

We are tender chunks of growing, reasoning, loving, self-moving life crawling over the patches of vegetation that cover a runty rock tumbling off to the side of an immense emptiness. And we will one day—a day not too far off, on the cosmic calendar—meet a power that rearranges the rock and the reasoning life that interrupted the nothingness for a moment. At that point we and all the value we do bring to the universe will be gone. From the cosmic perspective we should worry about this about as much as you would worry about a fish trapped in a tidepool: the fish couldn't do very much, anyway, and eventually it was going to die regardless. In the biggest scheme of things, the fish's situation is hardly a tragedy. But at the same time, we can still say that the fish matters. If it is only a small cost to

---

20. Just consider the panicky tone of Ecclesiastes 1:

"What profit have we from all the toil which we toil at under the sun? One generation departs and another generation comes, but the world forever stays. . . . Nothing is new under the sun! Even the thing of which we say, 'See, this is new!' has already existed in the ages that preceded us. There is no remembrance of past generations; nor will future generations be remembered by those who come after them."

you, you drag your heel through the sand to plow a release channel from the tidepool back to the sea. Similarly, while we do not matter very much on the cosmic scale, the norms that do apply to us come down on the side of making lives better: help a person instead of harming one. Beyond that, the picture of what to do and how to live fizzes up with a soothing effervescence. We are small and imperfect. Might as well enjoy seeing a sunset or tasting some ice cream or listening to a child laugh.

REFERENCES

Abramson, Kate, and Adam Leite. 2011. "Love as a Reactive Emotion." *Philosophical Quarterly* 61: 673–699.

Alpert, Avram. 2022. *The Good-Enough Life.* Princeton, NJ: Princeton University Press.

Aristotle. 1999. *Nicomachean Ethics.* 2nd ed. Translated and edited by Terence Irwin. Indianapolis, IN: Hackett.

Audi, Robert. 2005. "Intrinsic Value and Meaningful Life." *Philosophical Papers* 34: 331–355.

Ayer, A. J. 1990. *The Meaning of Life.* New York: Charles Scribner's Sons.

Baier, Kurt. 1957. "The Meaning of Life." Inaugural lecture delivered at the Canberra University College, October 15, Canberra, Australia.

Baier, Kurt. 1988. "Threats of Futility: Is Life Worth Living?" *Free Inquiry* 8, no. 3: 47–52.

Bardi, Jason Socrates. 2006. *The Calculus Wars: Newton, Leibniz, and the Greatest Mathematical Clash of All Time.* New York: Thunder's Mouth Press.

Bar-Lev, Amir, dir. 2017. *Long Strange Trip.* Season 1, episode 6, "It Becomes Everything." Aired May 25, 2017, on Amazon Prime.

Bateman, Jason, Sean Hayes, and Will Arnett, hosts. "Jon Stewart." September 27, 2021. *Smartless,* podcast. https://www.smartless.com/episodes/episode/236934e3/jon-stewart.

Bell, Macalaster. 2019. "On the Virtue of Taking Oneself Lightly." In *Oxford Studies in Normative Ethics,* edited by Mark Timmons, 161–182. Vol. 9. Oxford: Oxford University Press.

REFERENCES

Belliotti, Raymond Angelo. 2001. *What Is the Meaning of Human Life?* Amsterdam: Rodopi.

Belshaw, Christopher. 2005. *10 Good Questions about Life and Death.* Malden, MA: Blackwell.

Benatar, David. 2017. *The Human Predicament.* Oxford: Oxford University Press.

Bennett, James O. 1984. "'The Meaning of Life': A Qualitative Perspective." *Canadian Journal of Philosophy* 14: 581–592.

Blackburn, Simon. 2001. *Being Good.* Oxford: Oxford University Press.

Bradford, Gwen. 2015. *Achievement.* Oxford: Oxford University Press.

Bradford, Gwen. 2016. "Achievement, Wellbeing, and Value." *Philosophy Compass* 11: 795–803.

Bradley, Ben. 2006. "Two Concepts of Intrinsic Value." *Ethical Theory and Moral Practice* 9: 111–130.

Bramble, Ben. 2014. "On William James's 'Is Life Worth Living?'" *Ethics* 125: 217–219.

Bramble, Ben. 2015. "Consequentialism about Meaning in Life." *Utilitas* 27: 445–459.

Brogaard, Berit, and Barry Smith. 2005. "On Luck, Responsibility and the Meaning of Life." *Philosophical Papers* 34: 443–458.

Cahn, Steven M. 2008. "Meaningless Lives?" In *The Meaning of Life: A Reader,* edited by E. D. Klemke and Steven M. Cahn, 236–238. Oxford: Oxford University Press.

Calhoun, Cheshire. 2018. *Doing Valuable Time: The Present, the Future, and Meaningful Living.* Oxford: Oxford University Press.

Campbell, Stephen M., and Sven Nyholm. 2015. "Anti-meaning and Why It Matters." *Journal of the American Philosophical Association* 1: 694–711.

Camus, Albert. 2008. "The Myth of Sisyphus." In *The Meaning of Life: A Reader,* edited by E. D. Klemke and Steven M. Cahn, 72–81. Oxford: Oxford University Press.

Chappell, Timothy. 2007. "Infinity Goes Up on Trial: Must Immortality Be Meaningless?" *European Journal of Philosophy* 17: 30–44.

Coates, Ashley. 2022. "Awe's Place in Ethics." *Ethical Theory and Moral Practice* 25: 851–864.

Darwall, Stephen L. 1983. *Impartial Reason.* Ithaca, NY: Cornell University Press.

Dunkle, Ian D. 2019. "The Competition Account of Achievement-Value." *Pacific Philosophical Quarterly* 100: 1018–1046.

REFERENCES

Dworkin, Ronald. 2000. *Sovereign Virtue: The Theory and Practice of Equality.* Cambridge, MA: Harvard University Press.

Dworkin, Ronald. 2013. *Justice for Hedgehogs.* Cambridge, MA: Belknap Press.

"Edgar Mitchell's Strange Voyage." 1974. *People* 1, no. 6 (April 8). https://peo ple.com/archive/edgar-mitchells-strange-voyage-vol-1-no-6/.

Evers, Daan, and Gerlinde Emma van Smeden. 2016. "Meaning in Life: In Defense of the Hybrid View." *Southern Journal of Philosophy* 54: 355–371.

Feinberg, Joel. 2008. "Absurd Self-fulfillment." In *The Meaning of Life: A Reader*, 3rd edition, edited by E. D. Klemke and Steven M. Cahn, 153–183. Oxford: Oxford University Press.

Fischer, John Martin. 2020. *Death, Immortality, and Meaning in Life.* Oxford: Oxford University Press.

Frankfurt, Harry G. 1988. *The Importance of What We Care About.* Cambridge: Cambridge University Press.

Frankfurt, Harry G. 1999. "On the Usefulness of Final Ends." In *Necessity, Volition, and Love*, 82–94. Cambridge: Cambridge University Press.

Frankl, Viktor E. 1959. *Man's Search for Meaning.* Translated by Ilse Lasch. Boston: Beacon Press.

Garvey, James. 2011. "Diamonds in the Cosmic Sands." *Philosophers' Magazine* 54: 22–31.

Gewirth, Alan. 1998. *Self-Fulfillment.* Princeton, NJ: Princeton University Press.

Gilabert, Pablo. 2022. "Perfectionism and Dignity." *European Journal of Philosophy* 30: 259–278.

Glasgow, Joshua. 2020. *The Solace: Finding Value in Death through Gratitude for Life.* New York: Oxford University Press.

Glasgow, Joshua. 2023. "Death, Value, Gratitude, and Solace: A Response to Bradley, McAleer, and Rosati." *Journal of Philosophical Research* 48: 301–316.

Goetz, Stewart, and Joshua W. Seachris. 2016. "Introduction." In *God and Meaning: New Essays*, edited by Joshua W. Seachris and Stewart Goetz, 1–10. New York: Bloomsbury.

Gordon, Jeffrey. 1984. "Nagel or Camus on the Absurd?" *Philosophy and Phenomenological Research* 45: 15–28.

Grau, Christopher. 2006. "Irreplaceability and Unique Value." *Philosophical Topics* 32: 111–129.

Grau, Christopher. 2010. "Love and History." *Southern Journal of Philosophy* 48: 246–271.

REFERENCES

Grey, William. 1993. "Anthropocentrism and Deep Ecology." *Australasian Journal of Philosophy* 71: 463–475.

Griffin, James. 1986. *Well-being: Its Meaning, Measurement, and Moral Importance.* Oxford: Clarendon Press.

Hammerton, Matthew. 2022. "Well-being and Meaning in Life." *Canadian Journal of Philosophy* 52: 573–587.

Hare, R. M. 1972. *Applications of Moral Philosophy.* Berkeley: University of California Press.

Harrison, Jonathan. 1978. "The Importance of Being Important." *Midwest Studies in Philosophy* 3: 221–238.

Heathwood, Chris. 2005. "The Problem of Defective Desires." *Australasian Journal of Philosophy* 83: 487–504.

Hepburn, R. W. 1966. "Questions about the Meaning of Life." *Religious Studies* 1: 125–140.

Herrera, Hayden. 2002. *Frida: A Biography of Frida Kahlo.* New York: Perrenial.

Hirji, Sukaina. 2019. "Not Always Worth the Effort: Difficulty and the Value of Achievement." *Pacific Philosophical Quarterly* 100, no. 2: 525–548.

Homer, *The Iliad.* 1924. Trans. A.T. Murray. Cambridge, MA: Harvard University Press.

Hooker, Brad. 2008. "The Meaning of Life: Subjectivism, Objectivism, and Divine Support." In *The Moral Life: Essays in Honour of John Cottingham,* edited by Nafsika Athanassoulis and Samantha Vice, 184–200. New York: Palgrave Macmillan.

Huerta, Dolores. 2006. "Dolores Huerta at Seventy-Five: Still Empowering Communities." *Harvard Journal of Hispanic Policy* 18: 13–18.

Hughes, Nick. 2017. "Do We Matter in the Cosmos?" *Aeon,* June 29. https://aeon.co/essays/just-a-recent-blip-in-the-cosmos-are-humans-insignificant.

Hume, David. 1777. "Of Suicide." *Hume Texts Online.* https://davidhume.org/texts/su/

Hurka, Thomas. 1993. *Perfectionism.* Oxford: Oxford University Press.

Hurka, Thomas. 2011. *The Best Things In Life: A Guide to What Really Matters.* Oxford: Oxford University Press.

James, Laurence. 2010. "Activity and the Meaningfulness of Life." *Monist* 93: 57–75.

James, Simon P. 2015. "Why Old Things Matter." *Journal of Moral Philosophy* 12: 313–329.

REFERENCES

James, William. 1899. *On Some of Life's Ideals*. New York: Henry Holt and Company.

Jollimore, Troy. 2020. "Morality, Perspective, and Fantasy: A Comment on Sarah Buss." *Journal of Applied Philosophy* 37: 51–57.

Kahane, Guy. 2011. "Should We Want God to Exist?" *Philosophy and Phenomenological Research* 82: 674–696.

Kahane, Guy. 2014. "Our Cosmic Insignificance." *Noûs* 48: 745–772.

Kahane, Guy. 2017. "If Nothing Matters." *Noûs* 51: 327–353.

Kahane, Guy. 2022. "Importance, Value, and Causal Impact." *Journal of Moral Philosophy* 19: 577–601.

Kauppinen, Antti. 2012. "Meaningfulness and Time." *Philosophy and Phenomenological Research* 84: 345–377.

Kauppinen, Antti. 2016. "Meaningfulness." In *Routledge Handbook of the Philosophy of Well-Being*, edited by Guy Fletcher, 281–291. London and New York: Routledge.

Kekes, John. 1986. "The Informed Will and the Meaning of Life." *Philosophy & Phenomenological Research* 47: 75–90.

Keller, Simon. 2004. "Welfare and the Achievement of Goals." *Philosophical Studies* 121: 27–41.

Keltner, Dacher, and Jonathan Haidt. 2003. "Approaching Awe, a Moral, Spiritual, and Aesthetic Emotion." *Cognition and Emotion* 17: 297–314.

Kitcher, Philip. 2014. *Life after Faith: The Case for Secular Humanism*. New Haven, CT: Yale University Press.

Kolodny, Niko. 2003. "Love as Valuing a Relationship." *Philosophical Review* 112: 135–189.

Korsgaard, Christine M. 2018. *Fellow Creatures: Our Obligations to the Other Animals*. Oxford: Oxford University Press.

Korsmeyer, Carolyn. 2008. "Aesthetic Deception: On Encounters with the Past." *Journal of Aesthetics and Art Criticism* 66: 117–127.

Korsmeyer, Carolyn. 2016. "Real Old Things." *British Journal of Aesthetics* 56: 219–231.

Korsmeyer, Carolyn. 2019. *Things: In Touch with the Past*. Oxford: Oxford University Press.

Kristjánsson, Kristján. 2017. "Awe: An Aristotelian Analysis of a Non-Aristotelian Virtuous Emotion." *Philosophia* 45: 125–142.

Landau, Iddo. 2011. "The Meaning of Life *Sub Specie Aeternitatis*." *Australasian Journal of Philosophy* 89: 727–734.

Landau, Iddo. 2017. "Finding Meaning in an Imperfect World." Oxford: Oxford University Press.

Lenman, James. 2002. "On Becoming Extinct." *Pacific Philosophical Quarterly* 83: 253–269.

Levy, Neil. 2005. "Downshifting and Meaning in Life." *Ratio* 18: 176–189.

Luper, Steven. 2014. "Life's Meaning." In *The Cambridge Companion to Life and Death*, edited by Steven Luper, 198–212. Cambridge: Cambridge University Press.

Marek, Grant. 2021. "I Hiked to California's Mythical Giant Rock, the Purported Largest Freestanding Boulder in the World." *SF Gate*, April 9. Accessed October 26, 2021. https://www.sfgate.com/travel/edito rspicks/article/California-hike-Giant-Rock-Joshua-Tree-Landers-16087332.php?IPID=SFGate-HP-CP-Spotlight#.

Martela, Frank. 2017. "Meaningfulness as Contribution." *Southern Journal of Philosophy* 55: 232–256.

Matheson, David. 2016. "Creativity and Meaning in Life." *Ratio* 31: 73–87.

Mawson, Timothy. 2016. "What God Could (and Couldn't) Do to Make Life Meaningful." In *God and Meaning: New Essays*, edited by Joshua W. Seachris and Stewart Goetz, 37–58. New York: Bloomsbury.

McShane, Katie. 2018. "The Role of Awe in Environmental Ethics." *Journal of Aesthetics and Art Criticism* 76: 473–484.

Metz, Thaddeus. 2002. "Recent Work on the Meaning of Life." *Ethics* 112: 781–814.

Metz, Thaddeus. 2003. "Utilitarianism and the Meaning of Life." *Utilitas* 15: 50–70.

Metz, Thaddeus. 2013. *Meaning in Life*. Oxford: Oxford University Press.

Mill, John Stuart. 1971. *Autobiography*. Oxford: Oxford University Press.

Moller, Dan. 2007. "Love and Death." *Journal of Philosophy* 104: 301–316.

Moore, George Edward. 1903. *Principia Ethics*. London: Cambridge University Press.

Morioka, Masahiro. 2015. "Is Meaning in Life Comparable? From the Viewpoint of 'The Heart of Meaning in Life.'" *Journal of Philosophy of Life* 5, no. 3: 50–65.

Mulgan, Tim. 2015. *Purpose in the Universe: The Moral and Metaphysical Case for an Anthropocentric Purposivism*. Oxford: Oxford University Press.

Nagel, Thomas. 1971. "The Absurd." *Journal of Philosophy* 68: 716–727.

Nagel, Thomas. 1986. *The View from Nowhere*. Oxford: Oxford University Press.

Nietzsche, Friedrich. 1873. "Schopenhauer as Educator." Translated by Adrian Collins. Wikisource. Accessed November 3, 2021. https://en.wikisource.org/wiki/Schopenhauer_as_Educator.

REFERENCES

Nozick, Robert. 1981. "Philosophy and the Meaning of Life." In *Philosophical Explanations*, edited by Robert Nozick, 571–647. Cambridge, MA: Belknap Press.

Nozick, Robert. 1989. *The Examined Life: Philosophical Meditations*. New York: Touchstone.

Pascal, Blaise. 1958. *Pensées*. New York: E. P. Dutton & Co. Accessed December 18, 2018. http://www.gutenberg.org/files/18269/18269-h/18269-h.htm.

Persson, Ingmar, and Julian Savulescu. 2019. "The Meaning of Life, Equality, and Eternity." *Journal of Ethics* 23: 223–238.

Portmore, Douglas W. 2007. "Welfare, Achievement, and Self-sacrifice." *Journal of Ethics & Social Philosophy* 2: 1–28.

Powell, Sarah. 2016. "A Monument More Lasting than Bronze." *Folger Shakespeare Library*, March 8. https://www.folger.edu/blogs/collation/more-lasting-than-bronze/

Proudfoot, Ben. 2001. "She Changed Astronomy Forever. He Won the Nobel Prize for It." *New York Times*, July 27. https://www.nytimes.com/2021/07/27/opinion/pulsars-jocelyn-bell-burnell-astronomy.html.

Ramsey, Frank Plumpton. 1931. *The Foundations of Mathematics*. London: Routledge.

Rescher, Nicholas. 1990. *Human Interests*. Stanford, CA: Stanford University Press.

Rolston, Holmes, III. 1975. "Is There an Ecological Ethic?" *Ethics* 85: 93–10.

Routley, Richard. 1973. "Is There a Need for a New, an Environmental, Ethic?" *Proceedings of the XV World Congress of Philosophy* 1: 205–210.

Rowlands, Mark. 2015. "The Immortal, the Intrinsic, and the Quasi Meaning of Life." *Journal of Ethics* 19: 379–408.

Russell, Bertrand. 2008. "A Free Man's Worship." in *The Meaning of Life*, edited by E. D. Klemke and Steven M. Cahn, 55–61. 3rd ed. Oxford: Oxford University Press.

Sartre, Jean-Paul. 1946. "Existentialism Is a Humanism." Translated by Philip Mairet. Lecture. https://www.marxists.org/reference/archive/sartre/works/exist/sartre.htm.

Scanlon, T.M. 2000. *What We Owe to Each Other*. Cambridge, MA: Harvard University Press.

Scheffler, Samuel. 1982. *The Rejection of Consequentialism: A Philosophical Investigation of the Considerations Underlying Rival Moral Conceptions*. Oxford: Clarendon Press.

REFERENCES

Scheffler, Samuel. 2013. *Death and the Afterlife*. Edited by Niko Kolodny. Oxford: Oxford University Press.

Schlick, Mortiz. 2008. "On the Meaning of Life." In *The Meaning of Life: A Reader*, edited by E. D. Klemke and Steven M. Cahn, 62–71. Oxford: Oxford University Press.

Schmidtz, David. 2002. "The Meanings of Life." In *Robert Nozick*, edited by David Schmidtz, 199–216. Cambridge: Cambridge University Press.

Schopenhauer, Arthur. 2004. "On the Vanity of Existence." In *The Essays of Arthur Schopenhauer: Studies in Pessimism*, translated by T. Bailey Saunders. Project Gutenberg. https://www.gutenberg.org/files/10732/10732-h/10732-h.htm#link2H_4_0003

Setiya, Kieran. 2014. "The Midlife Crisis." *Philosophers' Imprint* 14: 1–18.

Sher, George. 2003. "On the Decriminalization of Drugs." *Criminal Justice Ethics* 22: 30–33.

Sigrist, Michael J. 2015. "Death and the Meaning of Life." *Philosophical Papers* 44: 83–102.

Simonton, Dean Keith. 1994. *Greatness: Who Makes History and Why*. New York: The Guilford Press.

Singer, Irving. 1992. *Meaning in Life: The Creation of Value*. New York: Free Press.

Singer, Peter. 1995. *How Are We to Live?* Amherst, NY: Prometheus Books.

Slote, Michael. 1989. *Beyond Optimizing: A Study of Rational Choice*. Cambridge, MA: Harvard University Press.

Smilansky, Saul. 2012. "On the Common Lament, That a Person Cannot Make Much Difference in This World." *Philosophy* 87: 109–122.

Smith, Michael. 2006. "Is That All There Is?" *Journal of Ethics* 10: 75–106.

Smuts, Aaron. 2013. "The Good Cause Account of the Meaning of Life." *Southern Journal of Philosophy* 51: 536–562.

Smuts, Aaron. 2018. *Welfare, Meaning, and Worth*. New York and London: Routledge.

Street, Sharon. 2006. "A Darwinian Dilemma for Realist Theories of Value." *Philosophical Studies* 127: 109–166.

Taylor, Richard. 1987. "Time and Life's Meaning." *Review of Metaphysics* 40: 675–686.

Taylor, Richard. 2008. "The Meaning of Life." In *The Meaning of Life: A Reader*, edited by E. D. Klemke and Steven M. Cahn, 134–142. Oxford: Oxford University Press.

Tiberius, Valerie. 2008. *The Reflective Life: Living Wisely with Our Limits*. Oxford: Oxford University Press.

REFERENCES

Trisel, Brooke Alan. 2004. "Human Extinction and the Value of Our Efforts." *Philosophical Forum* 35: 371–391.

Trisel, Brooke Alan. 2019. "How Human Life Matters in the Universe: A Reply to David Benatar." *Journal of Philosophy of Life* 9: 1–15.

Velleman, J. David. 2015. *Foundations of Moral Relativism*. 2nd exp. ed. Cambridge: Open Book Publishers.

Vitrano, Christine. 2020. "The Predicament That Wasn't: A Reply to Benatar." *Philosophical Papers* 49: 457–484.

Von Kriegstein, Hasko. 2017. "Effort and Achievement." *Utilitas* 29: 27–51.

Williams, Bernard. 2006. "The Human Prejudice." In *Philosophy as a Humanistic Discipline*, edited by Bernard Williams, 135–152. Cambridge: Cambridge University Press.

Wiggins, David. 1976. 'Truth, Invention, and the Meaning of Life', *Proceedings of the British Academy* 62: 331–378.

Wolf, Susan. 1982. "Moral Saints." *Journal of Philosophy* 79: 419–439.

Wolf, Susan. 2010a. "Good-for-Nothings." *Proceedings and Addresses of the American Philosophical Association* 85, no. 2: 47–64.

Wolf, Susan. 2010b. *Meaning in Life and Why It Matters*. Princeton, NJ: Princeton University Press.

Wolf, Susan. 2014. "The Meanings of Lives." In *The Variety of Values: Essays on Morality, Meaning, and Love*, edited by Susan Wolf, 89–106. Oxford: Oxford University Press.

Woodruff, Paul. 2014. *The Ajax Dilemma: Justice, Fairness, and Rewards*. Oxford: Oxford University Press.

INDEX

For the benefit of digital users, indexed terms that span two pages (e.g., 52–53) may, on occasion, appear on only one of those pages.

absurdists, 6
achievement, 58–61
Achilles, 4–5
Agent-Relative Symmetry, 67–68
Ali, Muhammad, 1, 5–6, 8–9, 10–11, 12, 26–27, 45, 56
Aristotle, 64–65

Benatar, David, 19, 48n.1
Bramble, Ben, 31–32, 33–34n.13, 36–37, 75–76, 77, 84n.22

Calhoun, Cheshire, 72n.8, 74, 86, 87n.26
Camus, Albert, 96, 98, 108–9
capacities. *See* Flourishing
Coltrane, John, 8–9, 22, 62–66, 82–83, 89–90
context, 15–17, 23
cosmic significance, 15–16, 23–26, 28–31, 41–43, 47, 49, 93–95, 100–1, 103–10

Dove. *See* Kahlo, Frida
Dworkin, Ronald, 94

escalation of value, 78, 80–81, 86–92

final value, 54–56, 58, 66–67
Fleming, Alexander, 18–19
flourishing, 62–66
Frankl, Viktor, 21–22, 45
freedom from the tyranny of value, 7, 103–10

Garcia, Jerry, 84

Hamming, Richard, 54–55
Hooker, Brad, 75–76, 77, 79–80
Horace, 2–3, 17–18, 105
Huerta, Dolores, 59–61, 82–83
Hybrid Theory of Meaning, 78–92

impact, 18–22, 60, 69–70, 85–86

121

irony, 96–98, 107–8
irreverence, 102–10

James, William, 17–18
Judge Learned Hand, 11

Kahane, Guy, 30–31, 32n.10,
33–34n.13, 38–39, 45n.28
Kahlo, Frida, 5–6, 10–11, 12–13,
14–15, 16, 55, 56, 70, 71, 72,
73–74, 78–79, 94–95
Korsmeyer, Carolyn, 34–35

Landau, Iddo, 12
Leibniz, Gottfried Wilhelm, 20–
21, 82–83
Lenman, James, 35–36
Levy, Neil, 80–81

Mandela, Nelson, 48–49
Metz, Thaddeus, 74, 80–81
Mill, John Stuart, 74–75, 77, 83–
84, 91–92
Mitchell, Edgar D., 99–100,
101–2, 104
monomania. *See* single-mindedness
Moore, G. E., 32–34
moral status, 10, 37–39, 60, 103–4
Mother Teresa, 74, 88

Nagel, Thomas, 15–16, 18–19, 96–
98
natural selection, 28–30
Newton, Isaac, 20–21, 82–83
Nietzsche, 64–65
nihilism, 6, 9–10, 96–99, 104

objective value, 27–28, 57, 73–81,
85–92, 96–99

objectivism about meaning, 74–
79
optimism, 7–8, 48, 95

Pascal, Blaise, 94–96, 99,
102–3, 109
personal interests, 48–53, 58–59,
60–66, 68, 105–10
pessimism, 6, 7–8, 25, 94–96
Plato, 22, 32–33, 37
potential. *See* flourishing
purpose, 44–47

Ramsey, Frank, 30–31
rarity, 15–16, 38, 62
recognition, 2–3, 8–9, 50, 95
relativism, 26–28
replaceability, 18–21

satire, 102–4
Schopenhauer, Arthur, 95–
96, 98
significance impulse, the, 1–6,
9–11, 12–13, 26–27, 45, 50–54,
55, 58, 59–60, 69–70, 95,
102–4, 109
single-mindedness, 4–6, 50,
81–82, 83
Smilansky, Saul, 100–1
social rewards, 50–52
Splinter. *See* Williams, Ted
subjectivism about meaning, 72–
74, 78–79
subjectivism about well-being, 56–
58, 73–74

threshold of objective value, 86–
92
Tolstoy, Leo, 2–3, 105

Index

tyranny of value. *See* freedom from the tyranny of value

Velleman, J. David, 56, 105

Welfarism, 31–34, 37–39

what could have been, 41–43

Williams, Ted, 1, 2, 5–6, 8–9, 12, 14–15, 16–17, 26–27, 45, 55, 56, 71, 72, 73–74, 78–79, 94–95

Wolf, Susan, 75n.13, 78–79, 79n.18, 87–88, 88n.29, 100n.8